CHALLENGE TO CHANGE

By the same author:

The Radical Kingdom
The Church
The Fair Face of Evil

Challenge
to
Change

A Radical Agenda for Baptists

NIGEL WRIGHT

KINGSWAY PUBLICATIONS
EASTBOURNE

Cover design by W. James Hammond

British Library Cataloguing in Publication Data

Wright, Nigel *1949*–
    Challenge to change.
    1. Great Britain. Baptist churches
    I. Title
    286.141

    ISBN 0–86065–566–0

Printed in Great Britain for
KINGSWAY PUBLICATIONS LTD
1 St Anne's Road, Eastbourne, E Sussex BN21 3UN by
Richard Clay Ltd, Bungay, Suffolk.
Typeset by Nuprint Ltd, Harpenden, Herts.

Dedicated to
the students of Spurgeon's College
in the hope that they might
take up the challenge

Contents

Foreword

Those who have never met the author of this book should be aware they are encountering a unique pedigree. Name another charismatic Baptist theologian with Restorationist and Anabaptist sympathies, who has written feature articles for the Guardian newspaper on the future of the Labour Party!

I warmly commend this stimulating and provocative book, not because I endorse every paragraph, but because it addresses issues of the day in pungent prose. In one chapter you will discover that for Baptists to oppose the disestablishment of the Church of England is a betrayal of the tradition they represent, and in another chapter the author presents cogent arguments for Baptist bishops—no easy task!

The publication of this book coincides with the commencement of my own ministry as General Secretary, and I would strongly encourage local churches and groupings of churches to use the book to inform their thinking on the Baptist identity debate. I guarantee you will disagree with some of the conclusions reached by the author. His description of the ideal church in Chapter 3 will lead some readers to be grateful this is not their local church. You may suspect that his love affair with the Restoration movement should really have ended in marriage. Some will conclude that Chapter 6 should have been written after he had served on the Baptist Union Council for a couple of years and that his comments on reforming the powers are unfair and out of touch.

Given these reservations, this could be an important and timely book which deserves a wide audience. It is hopeful in tone and clearly sees a renaissance of Baptist life in the coming years. I hope various groupings will use the book as a discussion point.

The contents of Chapter 2 could be developed as a theme for either a church conference or a series of workshops on the renewal of local church structures.

Those in ecumenical partnership should study that 'little understood and least popular' feature of Baptist life, the government of the local church, and face the charges of Chapter 4, that non-Baptists suggest we have a concept of church government which is unbiblical, unspiritual and impractical, and then go on to develop an apologetic for a Baptist understanding of church order.

Many involved in the structures of the Union (including Nigel!) will need to reflect thoughtfully on what he terms his most serious criticism, that 'the Baptist Union is an organisation which badly needs a theological overhaul...and the weakest part of the Baptist doctrine of the church concerns its national denomination structures'. Perhaps the commission he calls for will be one fruitful response to his challenge to change.

Nigel Wright's burden is to motivate Baptist Christians to address the central issue of what it means to be the church of Jesus Christ, with a costly invitation to examine with theological rigour those cherished understandings of our Baptist traditions. The best contribution Baptists may make to the Decade of Evangelism, is to renew their understanding of what it means to be the church and then express this with spiritually dynamic models.

David Coffey
General Secretary (from April 1991)
The Baptist Union of Great Britain

Preface

Between initiating and completing this work there took place several events or series of events which were bound to have a bearing on it. In the latter part of 1989 the Marxist countries of Eastern Europe, inspired by the promptings towards *glasnost* and *perestroika* in the Soviet Union, moved rapidly towards their long-awaited freedom and left the face of the continent startlingly transformed. In consequence a new if at first somewhat hesitant sense of hope for the future set in and began to show signs of applying for a permanent residence visa.

Then in July 1990 it was announced that the incoming Archbishop of Canterbury was to be Dr George Carey, Bishop of Bath and Wells. After the first surprise of this unexpected news, the decision was seen as an inspired and imaginative choice. As an evangelical with a keen theological mind and proven abilities as a leader and bishop, it was widely felt that Dr Carey could bring to the cause of the Christian faith in this country just what was needed. Prior to this, and in a less headline-catching fashion, it had been decided and announced that the new General Secretary of the Baptist Union as of its 1991 Assembly would be the Revd David Coffey, a former Union President. Together with the Revd Keith Jones as his assistant, he would lead the majority of British Baptists into the next decade and perhaps beyond. This popular decision itself followed hard on the heels of the strategic move of the Baptist Union headquarters to modern and well-equipped new premises in Didcot, Oxfordshire. It contributed to the already growing sense that Baptist Christians were in for a period of progressive and creative change which would parallel the similar changes taking place elsewhere among British Christians.

There is no doubt that the leadership that is given and the decisions that are made in the very near future will influence the life of Baptist Christians and their contribution to the Christian mission for a long time to come. It is essential that the best decisions are made. This is especially so as we make our contribution to a Europe that is in reconstruction and where potential for change is abroad.

This book may best be described, therefore, as a 'tract for the times'. This is one way of saying that it is far from perfect, that it will be found to contain particular points of view which will not always command support, that it is, in the best sense I hope, a polemical book. It is written, as the title suggests, in the expectation of change and as a conscious and unembarrassed attempt to influence the course of discussion and the flow of events. It has a certain robust character, therefore, although I hope never an unkind one. As a tract for the times it assumes that Baptists will be engaging in discussion about how they wish to organise their common life. It aims to be a stimulus to that discussion, since conversation is one of the highest forms of communication.

In writing this book I have enjoyed many and varied conversations around the themes it seeks to address. To list all my conversation partners would be tedious and possibly unhelpful since it might unfairly convey the impression that they share my opinions. I leave the names unrecorded in order to protect the innocent, but I am deeply grateful for the time spent by them knowingly or unknowingly in contributing to this enterprise. May the conversation continue!

Nigel G. Wright
Spurgeon's College
January 1991

I

On Being a Baptist

This is a book written by a Baptist for Baptists. Certainly I hope that others may want to read it. It should prove of interest to those who share Baptist convictions but are at present in non-Baptist churches; to members of restorationist churches; to those who belong to Baptist-minded churches which are not aligned with any major Baptist denomination; to Strict or Grace Baptists; and even to members of other established denominations who would like to find out what is going on in some other neck of the wood. But having said all that, it remains a book written by a Baptist for Baptists.

I am a Baptist. Over the twenty-five years since my conversion I have belonged to Baptist churches. I am an ordained and duly accredited Baptist pastor, was trained (among other places) in a Baptist college, have exercised ministry in Baptist churches, and am now a theological teacher in a Baptist college helping to train other Baptist pastors. Most Sundays find me preaching in some Baptist church somewhere in the country, or working in the local Baptist congregation of which I am an elder.

I have had to overcome certain obstacles before setting pen to paper (fingers to word-processor). One obstacle was wondering whether there would be a sufficiently large readership to make a book viable. Strangely, it seems easier to write for the charismatic, evangelical or restorationist markets than for the Baptist one. Perhaps they buy more books. Of course, all these markets overlap, but the question remains: who writes specifically for Baptists? Who feels that he or she has something to say to Baptist believers? The fact that Baptist churches in this country have in excess of a quarter of a million people in their communities, although not all in formal membership, ought on the face of it to provide a ready market. This is a substantial part of the believing population of the United Kingdom and so potentially a wide readership should be there.

A greater obstacle, however, was the thought that many of these people do not really think of themselves as Baptists. They consider themselves to be first and foremost Christians, and who can object to that? Possibly they may feel a primary bond of loyalty not to other Baptists but to other evangelical Christians, or to charismatics or (more vaguely but no less truly) to other 'live' churches. Hence the plain fact that when Baptists move they are more concerned to find a 'live' church than to find a Baptist one. If it happens to be Baptist and live, all well and good. But to be Baptist and bored is no fun for anyone. Of course the whole process works the other way too, and the majority of progressive Baptist churches are peopled by former members of other denominations.

I am not complaining about any of this. In fact I shall frequently refer in this book to 'Baptist Christians' as a way of indicating that being a Baptist is really a variation on a theme. The dominant theme for us all should be belonging to Christ and those who are his. The 'Baptist' bit is the expression of a conviction concerning what belonging to Christ involves, but the word 'Christian' is primary.

Analysed further, the obstacle looks like this: to talk about being a Baptist sounds old-fashioned and boring. When a new solidarity with others is being experienced and the ecumenical interchurch process is under way, to talk about Baptist values may sound defensive and reactionary, not to say divisive. It has overtones of justifying the system to which we belong, particularly if those who beat the Baptist drum might be thought to be after our money. It feels like obligatory propaganda issued for the sake of form or tribal loyalty. In brief, the 'Baptist bit' may seem plain dull compared with all the other things God is doing in our age.

Besides, to the popular mind, those who are most commonly perceived as being advocates of the Baptist cause may not always seem the best advertisement. In the experience of some, they are not always the most spiritually minded members of the congregation—although they might well be the most powerful. They seem to delight in bureaucracy and, when it comes to the church meeting, seem to be the most awkward of the lot! Is this what being a Baptist means? If so, can people be blamed for devaluing or even rejecting it?

This is where I have to say why I am writing this book. First of all the disclaimers: it is not because I am a Baptist by pedigree who feels obliged to do so. In these matters my family pedigree is highly dubious and is best summarised as post-Christian with Salvation Army antecedents and Quaker connections! What it has bequeathed to me is a distrust of the establishment and a suspicion that the radical minority is more likely to be right than the conformist majority. But certainly there is no sense of obligation.

Neither am I writing because I particularly like the Baptist system as it has been constructed, nor do I think that others should too. As it happens there appears to me to be much in the local churches, the denominational structures and in inherited attitudes and assumptions which is less than the best and is crying out to be radically altered.

On the other hand, neither am I writing because I have a personal axe to grind. The Baptist 'system' has been uniformly helpful and kind to me and has provided without hindrance many of the life opportunities that have come my way. I am grateful for the fine men and women who have been encouragers, mentors, colleagues and friends, and I look forward to serving with them and their kind for the rest of my life, God willing.

What, then, lies behind this book? It is the simple conviction that Baptist values and beliefs are right. When the founders of the Baptist movements gained their insights into the nature of the universal church of Christ and the ordering of the local church which is its expression, they were recovering something of great significance in which I passionately believe. Moreover, what they perceived was not of secondary importance but of the essence of the gospel itself. It had to do with the kind of disciples-in-community which Jesus intended to call into being, which the Spirit gathered on the day of Pentecost and which is more likely than anything else to be the means of changing the world.

The commitment reflected in this book therefore is not to denominational structures as such but to fundamental beliefs and values. The conviction that breathes through it is that recovery of these, understanding of them and confidence in them will aid spiritual life and health. Once recovered, it will be seen that these principles actually call the status quo into question and logically lead to the demand that substantial reforms take place.

It is for this reason that the title of the book is a true description of its content—it is a challenge to change. The intentions of the book are simultaneously conservative and radical. It is conservative in that it is drawing the reader's attention back in time to certain events and moments of insight which are considered to be crucial. In the first instance, these events are the dawn of the Anabaptist movement on the Continent in the 1520s (more details in chapter 9) and of the English Baptists in the first and subsequent decades of the 1600s. But these events are themselves only held to be significant because they themselves were inspired by even older events, namely the life, death and resurrection of Jesus and the emergence of the first community of his followers in the first century of the Christian era. The interest is not in Baptist origins for their own sake but in obedience to Jesus as this is illuminated by Baptist origins.

This essentially conservative interest is however believed to be of radical significance for today. The accumulation of power always brings its distortions. This is true in church bodies as elsewhere. Seen in the light of Jesus Christ, the present is judged and found wanting. The everpresent sinful tendencies which attend human persons and their institutions must constantly be brought back into line with the Lord they confess. Often, this message is not welcomed because it is felt to threaten and disturb—but it is necessary. It involves re-examining ourselves in the light of our roots and questioning what is. From a different historical context the words of Isaiah are appropriate here:

> Listen to me, you who pursue righteousness and who seek the Lord: Look to the rock from which you were cut and to the quarry from which you were hewn; look to Abraham, your father, and to Sarah, who gave you birth (Is 51:1–2).

Isaiah's point is true for us. We find our own identity and an understanding of God's purpose for us when we look to our own origins. Where we are going to has something to do with where we have come from. To examine our own origins is bound up with knowing who we are and what we must do in the here and now.

Some years ago I wrote a book which touched upon many of the themes which will re-emerge in this present study. I called it *The Radical Kingdom*. The book attempted to examine the teachings of the restoration movement which were gaining ground at that time. It contained words which were both appreciative and critical. After some years the restoration movement does not seem as threatening to the more established churches as it once did. This is no doubt due to greater understanding of it and to a softening of some of its more strident attitudes.

However, chief among the factors which have led to a new

mood must be that the movement is now old enough to realise that it too has problems. People leave restoration churches for new pastures because they are disillusioned and discontented, just as they leave the more historic churches. Even renewed worship can begin to seem boring and contentless after a time. The relentless activism of a new church can become wearing and exhausting and a more established, if less dynamic, church can seem attractive simply because it allows more human space. The intensity of the movement has its casualties not least when leadership teams fall out, churches disintegrate and revered figures show that they too are made of clay. When death takes elder statesmen, we are faced with the ultimate reminder of the limit of mortality which confronts all of us.

All these things lead to the more modest attitude which has long prevailed in older movements for the same reasons. Into this picture comes also the search for identity. When the excitement of being a pioneering venture has worn off, the question of who exactly we are looms large. The restoration movement is now facing this question.

Much of this book is about identity. I refer to the restoration movement because it seems to me that the question they face faces us all. Sometimes, what can be seen in sharp relief in a newer and simpler movement helps us to understand what is taking place in more complex forms in movements which are more established. Let us put it like this: every person faces the question of identity. Those who are secure in their identity, who know where they have come from and where they are going to, are more likely to live healthy and productive lives than those whose identity is in question. Identity serves as an anchor in the matrix of human life, enabling us to sense our part within it. The same is true of churches.

In recent decades much has happened within the church in this country. New churches and movements have come into being and older ones have experienced a measure of renewal. The sense of excitement, of spiritual springtime, has been in the air. Many of the newer churches have come to birth in a

climate of joyful exuberance and triumph, although difficulties are always to hand even for them. Yet with the
growth to maturity it becomes necessary to draw upon more
than the sense of excitement. Roots go down into the ground
and look for firmer soil into which to bed themselves. These
roots then draw life from the soil to nourish the growing plant.
Where there are shallow roots the plant remains vulnerable,
the rapid growth is fragile. What has come quickly into being
feels as if it could pass just as swiftly away. It is at this point
that the question of identity becomes crucial. We need to put
down our roots more firmly.

Every church needs to draw upon wider resources to sustain itself healthily. To maintain the life of a community over
a long period of time requires resources that can be appropri-
ately consumed. The sense of identity, of 'this is who we are
and what we are about', is part of this. It provides the param-
eters within which we live out our lives. Even the first church
in Jerusalem needed to draw upon a sense of history and
destiny to sustain its life. The resource for them was the
history of God's dealings in the Old Testament and the prom-
ise of future dealings. We hear Peter quoting from the
prophet Joel to explain the phenomenon of Pentecost (Acts
2:17–21). Later, we hear Stephen outlining the whole history
of Israel as the context for understanding what was happening
with the church and its preaching in the present (Acts 7).

For us also the Bible functions as the primary source for
understanding our identity. But we cannot ignore the almost
2,000 years of history that have passed since the Bible was
completed. We have a need to locate ourselves within the
varying streams of interpretation of the Bible which have
emerged over the years. All of this adds to our need for a
sense of identity and place.

It is not long, therefore, before any renewal movement
begins to draw upon its deeper sense of identity in order to
sustain itself. It searches for roots in the past. This is to be
observed in the tendency among renewed Catholics to

retrieve elements of spiritual devotion from their own tradition in a way which surprises renewed Protestants. The same tendency differently expressed is observable among the Ichthus stream of churches in London, finding nourishment in the Anabaptist movements of the sixteenth century and the Moravians of the eighteenth.

It is all to do with the search for identity in order to sustain the enterprise of the present. The sense that we are not alone in our pilgrimage, that others have trodden the way before us, acts both as an inspiration and a warning. By seeing how they overcame obstacles we are encouraged. By noting the mistakes they made or the characteristic difficulties they encountered, we may be forewarned in the present trials that confront us. All of this helps to sustain us in a journey which, once the initial excitements are over, appears more daunting and demanding than at first we imagined.

No doubt it is a symptom of advancing years, but the further I journey the more important becomes the question 'Where will I find the energy I need to sustain me in that which is yet to be?' I have no desire to become increasingly grey and bland with the passing of the years. I have not the slightest desire to pass into old age holding ever more rigidly to what I have previously known, living in the old grooves. What I do need is a creative sense of my own identity, and with it of my destiny, that the life that remains may be of innovative fulfilment of both. The same dynamic is present in churches.

Some time ago I was visiting a large and effective Baptist church. The Spirit had done some marvellous things and the resulting fruit was very considerable in every way. One of the concerns to emerge in a leaders' meeting was 'Who are we?' I recognised in that moment that churches also need a sense of identity, an anchor for their lives in the present. Of course it is entirely right to say that Christ is the anchor, he is our identity. But it is also true that we exist in a context, not a vacuum. A church always exists in a certain place at a certain time and this too is part of our identity. Knowing not only that we are the church but *how* we are to be the church is of great importance. It frees us to get on with the job.

At that time I understood that there is such a thing as a 'renewed Baptist' identity. Both these words are essential. To be renewed speaks of the work of the Spirit in making alive and new. Without the Spirit we are nothing: certainly, we are not the church. Renewal is vital. But the word 'Baptist' is also essential because it speaks of what the churches should look like and how they should have their existence. It speaks of an identity. Later I shall seek to outline the basic elements in this identity.

For restoration churches several options are available at the current time. Having come to the point where the question of identity looms, it is possible to seek identity in a close-knit group of mutually supportive fellowships who develop a common sense of destiny. This is not wrong so long as it is understood as a form of mutual service and does not become exclusive and a reason for subtle pride. As we shall see, there is everything to be said for existing in a network of supportive churches.

Another option is to gain identity from relationship with a personality or a cluster of personalities who give some personal definition to a church. Elsewhere I shall argue that supportive personalities are most helpful, but not if our identity is dependent upon them. The risk of their obscuring or confusing our devotion to Christ is too great (as Jesus himself indicated in Matthew 23:9–12 and as Paul hints in 1 Corinthians 3:1–9).

A further option is to gain identity from a theology which contributes to a church's self-understanding and which is clearly understood and held by its members. To be sure, this can degenerate into theological rigidity and sectarianism, but on the whole seems to me to be the best option. When combined with a sense of being in a network of similarly-minded churches, the potential for effective witness is multiplied.

What I am arguing in this book is that through the renewing

of the Spirit, Baptists need to undergo a theological renewal to re-appropriate and re-express the Baptist values which are at the basis of their life. This ought then to lead to a renewal of local churches and of wider denominational relationships. Were this to happen, Baptist churches would then have the benefits of spiritual life allied to a profound sense of identity and purpose. This would put them in an excellent position to further the mission which they are called by God to fulfil. The potential is exciting but the cost is the challenge to change.

Before getting down to business and suggesting what needs to happen and how it may be done, it is appropriate to attempt to outline what is at the heart of it all. What are the values and principles that need to be recovered and re-appropriated by Baptist Christians? What is this identity that needs to be renewed? Essentially, it is about a way of being the church. The Baptist way of being the church reflects insights which are integral to the gospel.

To rediscover them, we need to go back further than contemporary expressions of Baptist church life and denominational existence, which may have moved from the roots of our tradition. We must go back further even than the founding of the Baptist Union in the nineteenth century and its so-called 'Declaration of Principle'. Valuable though it is, it is nevertheless a relatively recent statement. To recover Baptist roots it is necessary to understand the emergence of continental Anabaptists in the sixteenth century and English Baptists in the seventeenth century. They emerged from a hotbed of spiritual ferment and from the press of historical circumstances in the wake of the Reformation with certain clear principles and insights which they believed to be faithful to the New Testament. Here we shall attempt to express those insights and to assess their relevance today.

In common with the Protestant movement in general, on whose radical wing they stand, Baptists acknowledge *the supreme authority of the Bible in all matters of faith and conduct*. I have already referred to the emergence of Anabaptists and English Baptists in successive centuries. The existence of an historical link between them is a much debated point. It is clear that there were some connections between Anabaptists and England in the sixteenth century and between Dutch Anabaptists and the English settlers who formed the first Baptist church in Amsterdam early in the seventeenth century. It does not appear to be the case, however, that the continental Anabaptists actually gave rise to their English counterparts. Rather, we are to think of two movements emerging in parallel, with the link between them being the Bible. Studying the Bible led them to similar conclusions about the nature of the church and baptism.

The Anabaptists grew out of the Reformation, with its rediscovery of the Bible as a living authority within the church to which all other authorities were to be made subject. The tradition of the church, therefore, and the cumulative thinking of her theologians, however valuable, were subject to the primary authority of the Bible. Whatever in the tradition or theology did not accord with the plain meaning of Scripture was to be rejected. The Anabaptists entered readily into this approach to understanding the ways of God.

The movement itself first emerged out of Bible study groups meeting in the city of Zürich. An early leader, Conrad Grebel, wrote, 'But after we took Scripture in hand too, and consulted it on many points, we have been instructed somewhat...'[1] Similarly, the English Baptists were to emerge from the early Puritan movement in which the authority of the Bible was already well established. This was an assumption with which they began and to which they adhered. It can be asserted firmly, therefore, that the primary authority of Scripture is fundamental to the Baptist way of being the church.

To say this emphatically is worthwhile. Of course, when we refer to the authority of the Bible, what is intended is that the authority of God in Jesus Christ is mediated through the earthly means of Scripture. The Baptist Union Declaration of Principle therefore states in its first article: 'That our Lord and Saviour Jesus Christ, God manifest in the flesh, is the sole and

absolute authority in all matters pertaining to faith and practice, as revealed in the Holy Scriptures...'[2] From this follow
several further conclusions.

First, it is impossible for a Baptist to appeal to Baptist
tradition as an absolute authority. The true Baptist Christian
recognises that *the Baptist tradition itself* teaches that tradition
is subject to Scripture. Practically, this means that Baptists
cannot and should not do things because they are the Baptist
thing to do, but because they are deemed to be biblical.
Neither can they object to the new and unfamiliar on the
grounds that it is not 'the Baptist way'. 'The Baptist way' is to
test all things by the Scriptures. The significance of this will be
observed at various points throughout the book.

A second conclusion concerns the use of creeds. Historically, the early Baptists were very keen on producing confessions of faith, yet they consistently rejected the idea of an
imposed creed. The role of the confessions was twofold. They
served so to outline their doctrines as to answer the charge of
heresy levelled at them by their enemies. By formulating
confessions they could demonstrate that they belonged to the
orthodox Christian faith. A second function has to do with the
question of identity which we have already been considering.
The need to identify for themselves where they stood and
what they believed was answered by detailed confessions in
which their positions were outlined and in this way they distinguished themselves from other ways of being the church.

But it is important to note that confessions have not generally been understood as credal formulae to which assent has
been demanded. The reason for this is that to do so would
conflict with the Scripture principle which we are discussing. It
would exalt the authority of a creed, which is another form of
tradition, above the authority of Scripture, depriving it of its
freedom to speak in ways not hitherto envisaged and depriving the churches of the freedom of interpretation. It is for this
very good reason that the Baptist Union Declaration of Principle quoted above goes on to affirm: '...and that each

Church has liberty, under the guidance of the Holy Spirit, to interpret and administer His (Christ's) Laws.'[3]

Now, admittedly, this is somewhat strangely worded. To speak of 'Christ's laws' in this way sounds strange to our ears, since we think of grace and truth coming through Jesus Christ, not laws (Jn 1:17). What it is trying to say, however, is that the authority of the Bible is a dynamic and a living authority among God's people. The Spirit speaks through it, and although it is possible to describe what we hear him saying (for example, by means of confessions) we are not in a position to give the last word on it. Once we think we have the last word, we have actually made our definition the final authority and deprived Scripture of what is rightfully its own. This leads to a third conclusion.

A truly Baptist understanding recognises that our understanding of Scripture is not complete. If the Bible is free to speak in new ways, if the Holy Spirit is free to point out things previously missed, if each church has liberty to hear the hitherto unheard, then we are far from being in a static position. If the tradition cannot be held to contain the sum total of necessary understanding then we are in a progressive, open-ended situation in which we cannot rest content with what we have known but must be open to being disturbed by new light on the truth. The early Baptists understood this well. Indeed, it was because of this attitude that the truth of believers' baptism could dawn.

In 1604, a separatist congregation was founded in the Old Hall in Gainsborough from which both the early Baptists and the Pilgrim Fathers were to emerge. The members of this church covenanted together 'as the Lord's free people...to walk in all His ways, made known or to be made known unto them, according to their best endeavours, whatsoever it might cost them, the Lord assisting them'.[4] It has been commented that this statement combines modesty and expectancy. They did not think that they had arrived but were willing to be faithful to what they had seen. It is the same spirit that is found in the hymn which says, 'We limit not the truth of God to our poor reach of mind,' with its refrain, 'The Lord hath yet more light and truth to break forth from his word.' These words are themselves based on a saying by John Robinson, one of the Pilgrim Fathers associated with the congregation at Gainsborough.

It is precisely the insight that the tradition is not complete, that there is more, that is the genius of the early Baptists. Later, I shall use this as a reason why Baptists should discerningly embrace charismatic renewal, because in it more light and truth has broken forth from God's word. To indicate this point here highlights the fact that the fundamental Baptist attitude to Scripture is itself radical and disturbing. It is by no means a cosy option, but holds surprises for us all.

This brings me to a fourth and final conclusion concerning the authority of Scripture. It is that Baptist Christians are essentially evangelical. It is impossible to be truly Baptist without being evangelical. A non-evangelical Baptist is a contradiction in terms. To speak about evangelical Baptists is tautology. This takes us into a wider debate about what is meant by 'evangelical'.

I use the term to indicate an intention to live under the authority of Christ as made known decisively in Scripture. It has to do with acknowledging the priority of the Scriptures for our knowledge of God. To be sure, there may be debates about what we find there and how we apply it. It is certainly out of place for one to legislate for another what must be found there, since this is to set ourselves up as the ultimate authority. Clearly also, integrity makes its demands. Once I cease to see in Scripture what others obviously see, there are implications for fellowship and allegiances. But the intention to live under the authority of Scripture is fundamental and can be the common ground on which many can meet even if they then disagree in good faith on matters of interpretation. In this sense Baptists are inherently evangelical and once they move away from this heritage, they lose their identity.

Acknowledgement of the authority of Scripture in this way leads on to a second conviction which characterises Baptists.

It is that *the true church of Jesus Christ is composed of believers and therefore baptism should be the sign of freely chosen faith.* This conviction is often known as the 'believers' church' or 'free church' principle and brings together a number of ideas.

One idea concerns what it means to be a Christian. Negatively it asserts that people are not made Christians by heritage or ritual. Membership of a group, whether that be a family group by birth or a church group by ritual initiation, does not guarantee salvation. No individual can rely on such membership for salvation. If they do they are no more than name-Christians who have never encountered the living God on their own account. Positively, the idea asserts that to be a Christian involves conversion, that is, a work of God in the individual resulting in a response of heartfelt repentance and faith leading to a transformed life. In this understanding of what it means to be a Christian, freely chosen discipleship is crucial. There is no great need here to argue for this understanding. It accords with the teaching of the New Testament and particularly with the words of Jesus in Luke 13:23–24:

> Someone asked him, 'Lord are only a few people going to be saved?' He said to them, 'Make every effort to enter through the narrow door, because many, I tell you, will try to enter and will not be able to.'

The point in Jesus' words is that we cannot expect to enter en masse into the kingdom of God, that is by virtue of membership of some people-group, whether that be the Jewish people, a family or a religious denomination. Entry to the kingdom is on an individual basis. The door is narrow not because the love of God is limited but because only one can enter at a time. There is no other way of gaining entry than by passing through one by one. This understanding is radically different from that which prevailed in Christendom when Baptist views emerged into the light of day. At that time salvation was believed to be in the gift of the established church and was appropriated through its religious rituals.

This brings us to a further idea. The church is not to be conceived of as an institutional organisation mediating salvation. Rather, it is a people, a gathering of those who have truly believed. The local church is a church of believers, a free church composed of those in whose hearts the work of salvation has been wrought. A further term used to describe this is 'the gathered church', meaning both those who have been gathered by Christ out of the world and those who gather with Christ in the midst.

Accordingly, a church to be a church does not require the approval of a state authority nor the legitimation of an ecclesiastical hierarchy. It needs only for Jesus Christ to be in the midst of his people according to the words of Jesus himself: 'For where two or three come together in my name, there am I with them' (Mt 18:20). This is essentially a simple idea of the church. It dispenses with the quasi-political, worldly idea of church which had prevailed for centuries in favour of a simplified and purified concept of community for which the first church in Jerusalem was the example: 'Those who accepted his message were baptised, and about three thousand were added to their number that day. They devoted themselves to the apostles' teaching and to the fellowship, to the breaking of bread and to prayer' (Acts 2:41–42).

Simple though it sounds, there was nevertheless a revolutionary power at work in the recovery of this concept, just as there had been a spiritually and socially revolutionary power in the first church. We shall take up this theme again but must for the moment examine a further idea implied in this concept, which is to do with baptism.

Once it is accepted that the church comprises those who believe, a further step becomes necessary. On what basis may baptism be administered to infants who are incapable of the kind of repentance and faith which makes a person a Christian? Baptist Christians have concluded that there is no basis in Scripture for infant baptism nor can an adequate theological basis be found for the practice outside of Scripture. Indeed, infant baptism obscures the vital truths that need to be emphasised, because it affirms that salvation is indeed a question of belonging to the right group. It asserts that salvation is assured by virtue of membership in a particular family or religious body, thus allowing people to rest complacently on what others do for them rather than on their own responsible decision.

Underlying the rejection of infant baptism is a particular concept of grace. God is gracious to all but the grace that leads to salvation is one that engages us in a relationship. Saving grace is not infused as though it were a substance. It is not automatically conferred by sacramental action through baptism and eucharist. For grace to become operative in the inner life of men and women requires from them the response of faith. Indeed, it is by the grace of God that such faith is awakened in the first place, but it is awakened in order that, through the bond of faith, the grace that brings salvation may take hold of the inner life. Therefore where there is no faith, baptism lacks both its proper meaning and power and is not appropriate. The baptism of infants unprepared as yet for such faith is a distortion of the meaning of baptism.

Whatever it is (and there is no lack of attempts to justify it) such baptism is not New Testament baptism. Anabaptists and Baptists felt themselves compelled to be truly baptised and in so doing brought upon themselves the accusation of being 'Rebaptisers' (which is what 'Anabaptist' literally means) and the persecution of the establishment which they were conscientiously undermining.

It is still true to say that the Baptist conviction at this point is sharply criticised by some. It is particularly felt that it smacks of excessive individualism, that it atomises the church into a collection of private persons and loses the sense of its corporate nature. The focus, we are told, is directed to the response of the believing individual rather than the grace of God which takes the initiative. Baptists stress the subjective rather than the objective. What Baptists consider to be the weakness of infant baptism, its lack of emphasis upon the response in repentance and faith, is deemed by its proponents to be one of its great virtues. It speaks, we are told, of the grace of God showing that his saving love for us is not dependent on our love for him.

Baptists are able to affirm all of this, but none the less affirm that baptism in the New Testament is about human response to God, and functions as 'the pledge of a good conscience towards God' (1 Pet 3:21). It was and remains primarily the expression of repentance and faith, whereas the gift of the Spirit was recognised as the expression of God's action towards humans. For this reason the practice of infant baptism struggles to find a foothold in the New Testament. Even the argument from family solidarity fails to carry the weight of centuries of practising infant baptism. The idea that a child qualifies for baptism through membership of a Christian family explains the place of the child within the circle of faith without going on to justify the further step that he or she ought therefore to be baptised. Baptists insist that truly Christian baptism must be the expression of faith.

The arguments on this issue continue between believers who otherwise have much in common but the infant baptist case always suffers from the disadvantage of sounding like justification of a practice that people are unwilling, on grounds other than the theological, to dispense with. Those other grounds, I suspect, are an instinctive awareness that to abandon infant baptism logically leads to a different concept both of church and society. Infant baptism continues to function as a bond between the established church and society at large. There is the fear of stepping out beyond the secure confines of establishment religion (not just in the Church of England) to take up a more radical position. Infant baptism is therefore rationalised and retained.

It is usually possible to find a theology for a practice to which one is attached. The theological imagination is immensely creative. What infant baptists must succeed in doing, however, if they are to counter the Baptist case, is prove either that infant baptism was a New Testament practice (and it is generally acknowledged now that it was not) or that it is theologically necessary. To find a theology for it is one thing; to find a theology which renders it necessary is another.

All that infant baptists want to affirm about the love of God for children, their place within the community of the church, the privileges of belonging to a Christian family, the responsibility of Christian nurture, can be adequately expressed without the use of baptismal water. The Baptist practice of bringing newborn children for blessing and the dedication of their parents adapts itself well to all of these themes without distorting New Testament baptism. What makes it *necessary* to baptise infants?

I do not mean to say in all this robust language that believer baptists have nothing to learn. More attention must be given in particular to understanding and affirming the place of children in the church community. Strangely, Baptists have often held confused ideas about what baptism is, when it should occur, what is expected to happen, how it relates to membership and so on. Work needs doing in these areas. At the same time, the relative health of many Baptist churches throughout the world has more than a little to do with the clear way in which believers' baptism portrays the nature and the demand of Christian discipleship. It functions evangelistically as a sharp cutting edge with great power. It is often understood and appreciated by unbelievers because it is viewed as a responsible action, not compelled but freely chosen. It is a sharp weapon in the armoury and always has been. For the believer baptist, the infant baptist is missing out on a very great blessing.

It is not that the full immersion of a person makes a bigger impression. As it happens, the mode of baptism, whether by full immersion or the pouring of water on the head is not the real point. Anabaptists and Baptists actually baptised according to both forms on occasions, with the Anabaptists leaning towards pouring and the Baptists towards immersion. To say that Baptists believe in adult baptism by immersion, as is sometimes done, is not sufficiently accurate. They believe in believer (not necessarily adult) baptism (not necessarily by immersion). Immersion may be the preferable mode of baptism because of its rich symbolism, but it is freely chosen faith which is the key element.

Our attention now moves to a third basic principle of Baptist conviction, namely, *the priesthood of all believers and the autonomy of the local church.* By the first of these we mean the conviction that every believer has access to the Father through the Son in the Spirit. This direct access removes the need for specially appointed persons exercising a form of priesthood, that is, of mediation between God and the people. The ideas characteristic of the Roman Church, that by appropriate ordination a grace is conferred upon special persons to actualise certain realities, particularly the granting of absolution from sins and the transformation of the bread and wine during the eucharist into the body and blood of the Lord, are rejected as having no New Testament foundation.

The same ideas are, of course, present in the Anglican Church, despite the fact that there is a broader span of opinion about these things. The Church of England has never quite made up its mind whether it is presbyterian after all. Notions of priesthood are reinforced in such traditions by the wearing of vestments and other forms of clerical garb to emphasise the apartness of the priestly elite and by the use of honorific titles to reinforce notions of hierarchy (which literally means the 'rule of priests').

This entire ethos is considered by Baptists to be at variance with the teaching of Jesus and of the early church. Their conviction concerning the local church is rather that:

> a gospel church is an organized body of baptized believers equal in rank and privileges, administering its affairs under the headship of Christ, united in the belief of what he has taught, covenanting to do what he has commanded, and co-operating with other like bodies in Kingdom movements (G. W. McDaniel).[5]

This notion is not a denial of the fact that some members of the church are called to specific ministering functions as pastors, teachers, evangelists and so on. It does affirm that there are no functions which are exclusively the preserve of some and that the functions of some are also the responsibility of all. Pastors, teachers and evangelists, for instance, are necessary for the equipping of all in the work of pastoring, teaching and evangelism. There are implications in all of this for the kind of worship in which Baptist congregations will engage. It will be participatory, simple in construction and accessible to ordinary people.

A further conclusion from the priesthood of all believers concerns the government of the church. If all have access to God this confers upon each person a measure of competence to determine what the will of God may be and upon the gathered church a corporate competence in this area. This is generally referred to as the 'autonomy of the local church' and is where the concept of the church meeting finds its place. A chapter will be devoted to this topic because it appears to be in practice one of the most vulnerable points of the Baptist way of being the church.

Suffice it to say here that because believers have access to the mind of God, it renders the local church competent to discover for itself what it needs to know to direct its own affairs aright. It does not require to defer to a higher authority in these matters or to be told what to do, although should it choose to consult others because it is conscious of its lack of wisdom, it is entirely free to do so. To be competent does not mean being omnicompetent or omniscient and the wise church recognises this.

These insights into the nature of the church will need to be carefully examined and I will attempt to do so in the chapter entitled 'The Centre of Gravity'. The title is aptly chosen because this area is indeed very central. Churches which practise believers' baptism and believe in the believers' church are not truly Baptist unless they come to terms in some way (and there may be a variety of ways of doing so) with this dimension of church life. On the other hand, I shall argue in the

proper place that many Baptist churches are practising a distorted version of this principle and need to change very considerably before they are living up to their true principles.

We come to a fourth and final principle, which is the
principle of *freedom of conscience and the separation of
church and state*. By anybody's reckoning this must be considered supremely important. The belief that an individual is
responsible to God and that it is wrong for any outside authority, whether political or ecclesiastical, to interfere in genuine matters of conscience was learned the hard way. The first
Anabaptists, for instance, found themselves caught between
two demands, the demand of conscience by which they had
become persuaded that obedience to the Scriptures required a
certain form of church life, and the demands of the state which
told them they could not do what they felt obliged to do.

Out of this dilemma arose the conviction that the state had
no mandate to forbid what God had commanded and therefore the law of the land had to yield to the law of conscience.
Conscience was higher than law. This revolutionary principle
(well attested of course in the New Testament as in Luke
20:25 and Acts 5:29) effectively put a limit to the authority of
the state and was the denial of all totalitarianism. The power
of the state was only relative. The conscience was free. For
this conviction those who were convinced of it paid in blood,
but in so doing their blood became the seed of the civil
liberties which are now the birthright of many.

An extension of this was the insight that the ancient alliance
between church and state was wrong since its effect was to
encourage the church to use the power of the state to impose
its will and deny conscience. The roots of the alliance go far
back into history. Once the Roman Empire realised that it
could not defeat the church, it sought an alliance with it and
under Emperor Constantine and his successors Christianity
became, in the fourth century, the civil religion of the Empire
in a formal union. The Empire was seeking to use this religion
in the way it had used others, as the way of uniting the Empire
with a common creed.

After years of persecution, this change seemed to the church like the arrival of the millennium. Progressively the church began to use the power of the state to compel religious conformity. The temptation was a subtle one, and in different forms is still present with us. To back righteousness with power seems like doing the will of God. In the event, this move led to the steady corruption of the church and its transformation into an organisation far removed from the spirit of Jesus. The Baptist concept of the church was such that it required a new approach, disengaging the church from the state and allowing it to be again what it had been in the beginning, a community whose only power was in the quality of its life and the authority of its teaching.

These various ideas and principles, taken together, constitute a distinctive understanding of how to be the church. When looked at in principle they are compelling and attractive. Many who do not belong in the Baptist stream of thought might read of them and say, 'This is very much the way I think.' Indeed, many churches of all denominations increasingly reflect the principles outlined here. Necessity, in the form of a secularised society, has deprived the church of much of its privilege and position. There is always a tendency to make a virtue out of necessity and claim that we prefer it this way anyway! The fact is that the free church principle has had a powerful influence even on those church bodies which once rejected and opposed it. The sense of it has become more obvious with the passage of time and it has gained acceptance.

But the opposite has also happened. With increasing respectability and prosperity, radical Baptist thinking has accommodated itself to the establishment, adopting its attitudes and style, betraying its heritage. This book, written by a Baptist Christian for Baptist Christians, is not a challenge to change from our basic principles but to change so that we truly recover them and embody them in the world of today. It is a call for us to be ourselves.

2

An Agenda for Baptist Christians

This book is written out of the conviction that Baptist churches as they presently exist need to be transformed. Yet it is an entirely legitimate question to ask 'What are we supposed to change into?' Change of itself is of no great value; indeed, it can be destructive. There needs to be the assurance that what we are changing into is worthwhile, otherwise why bother? The intention of this chapter is to set out an agenda for change. An agenda is a list of things that have to be acted upon. This chapter seeks to indicate what those things are.

The first church of which I was a member was situated in an inner-city area of Manchester. My family background was such that church attendance was not a regular feature of life. We were lapsed nonconformists, but the church to which we did not go (if you understand my meaning) was the local Baptist church. We were connected to it by vague feelings of loyalty, occasional attendance at Sunday School and some affection for the people. When, in my teenage years, I was converted, this church did not provide a particularly inspiring beginning to the Christian life.

The building was large, badly maintained and looked like a warehouse. The attendance was minimal. Worship services were dull, sombre affairs, lacking any kind of warmth. For most of the church members religion appeared to be very much a matter of routine, although there were those who were patently sincere, if somewhat vague in their beliefs. Contact with other Baptist churches quickly revealed that there were others in similar condition. There was little sense of expectancy or of evangelism. Zeal was treated as though it were an embarrassment.

I say none of this to be unkindly critical. I conceived in those days an awareness that the church of Jesus Christ was not supposed to be as I had found it. It had to change. Fortunately, things have been looking up ever since, although the picture of church life I have just painted is still more common than is desirable. The wind of change and the breath of renewal have nevertheless been altering the face of the church. A young person coming to faith today is likely to find a very different atmosphere. But the need for change is still there.

The tragedy is that some churches have yet to see this. They are wedded to the past and conceive of their task in maintenance terms. They must maintain what exists and keep it going. The 'need to keep the doors open' is a phrase that I first heard at an early stage. Maintaining the institution rather than converting the world is the paramount concern.

Unfortunately, this then leads on to a particular concept of growth. The growth of the church is desired in order that other people may come and help us maintain the institution, keeping it going as it has always been. Everybody wants the church to grow, but people desire growth for different reasons. Some want it in order to keep the institution alive. Others see that the institution is an obstacle to faith and that it must die in order for growth to take place.

The key element in this is vision. Where there is no vision the people perish. Those whose vision is only retrospective, who insist on looking back to what used to be, will never take on board the challenge of change. Hindsight has a way of romanticising the past and making it into something it never was. In order to keep in touch with the past it is necessary that the rituals of the past are repeated in the present. This feature is true of the whole of life but it appears to be particularly true of religion. Because religious experience is associated with particular places, or is mediated through particular words or music, there is a tendency to preserve these things for the sake of the experience. Hence people have fierce attachments to liturgical forms, styles of music, church architecture, furniture or organisations. These are tied up with the sense of the holy which has inspired or sustained faith. All of this is perfectly understandable. At the same time it can become thoroughly selfish and incredibly narrow.

The true perspective for the Christian and the church is not backward- but forward-looking. Only when our vision is of things yet to be can we avoid the restricting and spiritually destructive attitudes which have been described. There is certainly much to be learned from the past, but the past cannot be altered. Only the future which has yet to be lived can be changed. It is essential that the church of Jesus Christ should lift up its head towards the future and the Lord who comes to meet it from the future.

What is our vision of the things that have yet to be? When our vision of the future is clear, something else clarifies. It is that the church as it presently exists must give itself in sacrifice for the future. What presently exists in the church must not be held on to, but rather given up for the sake of the vision that we pursue. To find itself, the church must lose itself. Whenever it seeks to 'save its own soul' by preserving the status quo, it begins to lose itself.

The church finds itself not by maintaining the past, but by sharing with God in his giving of himself for the sake of the world. It is in losing its identity that it finds its identity. It moves towards the future and is prepared to amend its life in the present, so that only that which serves the future is retained. As our vision for the future is so important, it is necessary in this chapter to spell out what it might look like and what its implications for the present shape of church life might be.

Spelling out a biblical vision

The vision must of course be rooted in the Bible. Scripture is our source of the knowledge of God and his purposes. We have already seen that for Baptist Christians it is the authority for all matters of faith and conduct. Happily, the Bible is a visionary book. It is certainly aware of the past and of how God's actions in the past directly affect the present. But it is filled from beginning to end with the sense that God has a great purpose and that he is moving the world towards its fulfilment. We might say that the Bible, in different ways in its various parts, puts before us an ultimate, a penultimate and an immediate vision.

The ultimate vision

This is as big as anything can be. It involves nothing less than all things and is described in Ephesians 1:9–10 as follows:

> And he made known to us the mystery of his will according to his good pleasure, which he purposed in Christ, to be put into effect when the times will have reached their fulfilment—to bring all things in heaven and on earth together under one head, even Christ.

These words are so disarmingly brief that it would be easy to miss their staggering implications. The purpose of God, according to Paul, which has now been revealed in the gospel, is to bring *all things in heaven and on earth together under one head, even Christ*. It is cosmic in scope. God is working towards the final unification and harmonisation of all things in Christ, causing all things that exist to find their true place in the universe in harmony with Jesus Christ. Christ, we are told, is the creative agent of all things visible and invisible (Col 1:18). He is the sustainer of all (Heb 1:3) and the reconciler of all (Col 1:19–20). He is in every way the mediator between God and humanity (1 Tim 2:5).

In the fulfilment of God's purposes, it is through Christ that the present creation will be transformed into the new heaven and new earth which is the home of righteousness (2 Pet 3:13). In every way Christ must be seen as the key who unlocks our knowledge of God (Jn 1:1), our perception of the universe (Jn 1:3–4) and our understanding of salvation (Jn 1:10–14). The Christian's vision of the future is one which sees the whole horizon being filled with God in Christ (1 Cor 15:28).

The implications of this vision are all-embracing. It involves the reconciliation of individuals to God through Christ (2 Cor 5:16–21). On the *personal level*, God engages his creatures in a relationship with himself which means that the gulf of alienation is crossed, that people are enabled to know that they are forgiven and accepted. In turn, this leads to the discovery of meaning and direction so that life may be lived creatively and purposefully. But salvation does not stop here and it is a mistake to imagine that it does.

On the *bodily level*, salvation includes the resurrection of the body, that is to say, a future event which transcends death, when human beings will experience a restoration to full embodied identity in the kingdom of God (Rom 8:11). In the light of this, no truly Christian theology can despise the body in the here and now. Because it is included in salvation, my own body and the bodies of others must be respected and cared for.

On the *cosmic level*, future salvation embraces more than the individual identities of human persons. It includes the context in which we live. This means that there is a future for the natural world. It too, in its own way, will be redeemed. Exactly how this will be and what it means we do not know. The apostle Paul, however, speaks of creation eagerly anticipating its future liberation from decay and groaning as in the labour pains of childbirth (Rom 8:18–21). The Christian hope of salvation must be understood as a universal hope in the sense that it sees the whole of the cosmos participating in salvation.

This does not mean that the cosmos will remain unchanged. Neither does it mean that there is no such thing as judgement. We are to think of the world being purged of those discordant distortions which we call sin and evil. In the true sense these do not belong to God's good creation but are distortions of what he has made. The biblical passages which look forward to a final conflict, or a catastrophic purging of creation (see, for example, 2 Peter 3:10–11), should be understood as the action of God in removing from the creation that which does not truly belong to it. The goal of this is to produce the new heaven and earth in which all things are fully indwelt by God in Christ through the Spirit (Rev 21).

This glorious vision of the fulfilment of all things visible and invisible in Christ has been called the 'christological omega'. It is the end-point to which all things are moving and being moved. It is a profoundly moving picture and, once grasped, has the power to motivate our living in the present. In the light of this vision, of the glory which is to be revealed, what sacrifice is too great? And how can we cling nervously to the relics of the past when such a vision beckons us to live dangerously in the present for the sake of the future? In the light of this vision, the petty, restricted nature of much contemporary church life is exposed. A healthy dose of this ultimate vision for all things is a necessary antidote to the shortsighted, small-minded attitudes which, sadly, are found among us.

The penultimate vision

So much for the ultimate vision. Is there a penultimate vision? To put it another way, do we have to wait for history to run its course, or is there anything to hope for before the end? It would be sad indeed if there were not. After outlining the vision for all things in Ephesians 1, the apostle Paul switches his attention in chapter 2 to the church. This is not accidental. What God wills to do in all creation he is already doing in the church. The church exists in the world as the sign of the purpose which God is working out in all creation.

In Ephesians 2, therefore, Paul speaks of the way in which by grace individuals have entered into salvation through faith. It is a question of before and after. Once we were dead in sins (v1), enslaved to dark powers and the ways of the world (v2), slavishly following the demands of our unchanged lives and subject to the wrath of God (v3). But because of the love, grace and power of God we have been raised from spiritual death into the life of Christ and created for good works (vv6–10). Every Christian believer who is being renewed by God is therefore a sign of the renewing work that God is doing in all creation. It begins with us.

Moreover, the Christian community is the sign of the saving activity of God. In this same chapter, Paul goes on to speak about how, in Christ, the 'dividing wall of hostility' (v14) which separates Jews and Gentiles on racial grounds is being removed to create 'one new man out of the two' (v15). The sign of God's activity in the world is not therefore individuals alone, but a new community, a new humanity in the midst of the old. To grasp this is crucial. There is a community of people in the midst of human communities in whom God is making his dwelling place (vv19–22). This community, known as the church, is the sign and demonstration of the saving activity of God which has all the world in view.

This is a very high view of the church. It explains why a book like this is worth writing. The implications of Paul's teaching are great. He affirms, for instance, that the purposes of God come to expression in a social reality, that is a specific community. The nature and behaviour of this social group can validate or invalidate the work of God. If this community does not live as the reconciled community, the people chosen out of the world to be transformed in their relationship to God and their fellows, it can hardly be the sign of the saving purpose of God. It might prove to be a sign of the failure of God, not his power to save. If this group appear to be no better than the rest of humanity, in what sense can they be a sign? If they show no evidence of access to the grace which changes lives and brings peace, how is the transcendent God present in them?

Furthermore, this community appears to be central to the purposes of God. It is not merely one of several irons in the fire which God has, but the focal point (though not the only point) of his activity on earth. In Paul's language:

> His intent was that now, through the church, the manifold wisdom of God should be made known to the rulers and authorities in the heavenly realms, according to his eternal purpose which he accomplished in Christ Jesus our Lord (Eph 3:10).

The church, then, is the community through which it is God's purpose to make known his wisdom and plan in the midst of human affairs. The plan of God centres upon the church. It is no wonder that Paul then goes on to pray for the church to be filled with the love of God and to say 'to him be glory in the church' (Eph 3:14–19). The church is the community in whom the glory of God is to be made visible. As the glory of God was known in the physical Temple of the Old Testament (2 Chron 7:1–3) and in the bodily temple of Jesus (Jn 1:14), so it is to be made known in the living temple of the church, composed of the lives of those who believe (Eph 2:22).

Now, it is quite clear from this that God has taken a great risk. We may wonder at the fact that God has taken great care to secure the salvation of humanity. He has himself come among us in the person of Jesus, dying and rising to restore us to himself. He has poured out the Spirit. All of God is involved in the work of salvation. And yet, he has taken the risk of entrusting the gospel to his church and making the fulfilment of his plan dependent upon its response to his call. It might be felt that at this point the plan of salvation could be derailed, not with the failure of God but of the church which he has called into partnership.

The history of the church suggests that it has not only failed to fulfil its vocation but has done so with abject distinction, being in its life a contradiction of the gospel it proclaims. At this point we might either despair or be utterly amazed at the humility of God in condescending to use such a church and at his faithfulness in not forsaking it. If there is a penultimate vision however, something to hope for as a sign that the ultimate vision is on its way to fulfilment, it is that the church might rise to fulfil its destiny and to become, substantially if not completely, that community of redeemed persons in which the glory of God may truly be seen.

That Paul holds fast to this vision is indicated in Ephesians 4. It must be said that Paul was no romantic when it came to the church. The New Testament records the various disappointments that he experienced in his ministry. He himself knew what it was to be hurt by his fellow-believers. He had seen their faults and failings and had known the pain of disappointment when Christ was not truly formed within them. It is not, then, as a starry-eyed idealist that he speaks in chapter 4 of the church coming to its proper place. He sees it growing up 'into him who is the Head, that is, Christ' (v15).

For Paul this means a number of things. It means stability in the truth as the church holds to its faith with conviction, clarity and honesty (v14). It means unity in the faith as believers deal with each other lovingly and patiently (vv2–6, v13). It means maturity as they grow in the knowledge of the Son of God (v13). And it means flexibility and fruitfulness as each part of this living body is involved in self-giving service (v12, 16). This is indeed a vision of a community to be reckoned with. It is not that it exercises great human and worldly power but that it brings into human life an embodiment of the loving and merciful power of God as revealed in Jesus Christ. In truth and grace it represents the Lord of the church in space and time, reflecting him and doing his work.

It must be admitted that in the face of the actual facts of the church it requires a leap of faith to believe that this vision is realisable. Stability, unity, maturity and flexibility may be found in some measure in all churches, but not to the degree that one might reasonably expect of the redeemed. Some churches do exhibit these qualities more than others and exist as true signs of the reconciling work of God. To become real in others will require the kind of far-reaching changes for which we shall be arguing shortly.

However, the faith of the believer is not so much in the church as in its Lord and in the fact that he who began a good work will bring it to completion. The risk-taking God who has included the church in his plan knows what he is doing. As the ultimate plan of God is a vision set before us in the future, so the penultimate vision of a mature church is a future reality towards which we are moving in human history. It is God's purpose to bring it to pass.

For the time being, the church is not so much God's building as his building site. The work is still in progress. To watch a building being erected is instructive. It is not a pretty sight. The work seems to take for ever as the foundations are laid, the structure erected, the roof put on. At this stage the work may seem painfully slow, but it is necessary. Then suddenly, the work seems to move very quickly as the outside appearance is completed, the roads covered and the gardens landscaped. All of a sudden, a fine building is standing there. So it may be with the church as it rises to become what had been in the mind of its Creator from the beginning. Even so, we are not here speaking of perfection but of the church becoming in substance, though with blemishes, what it has the capacity to be.

The immediate vision

This brings us to another area. In the light of the ultimate and penultimate visions as outlined, a third vision emerges. It is an immediate vision of what must happen beginning from now if the greater visions are to be fulfilled. The visions of which we have spoken cast their light into the present. If they remained in the indefinite future, they would not be visions but mirages never to be attained. Instead, they are true and meaningful visions which we are called to pursue as from today.

It is for this reason that, having outlined the broad picture in the earlier chapters of Ephesians, Paul goes on to draw out their implications for church life as it is lived here and now. We are not to be shaped by the past realities we have known but by the future towards which we move. In Ephesians 4:17

he begins to expound the practical application of what we have said, namely to live in all things according to Jesus Christ (Eph 4:20–21). This theme takes him into the areas of speech, attitude, worship and relationships in the family and in society, in all of which areas he spells out what it means to live according to Christ and in the power of the Spirit (4:17—6:9).

Paul's visionary logic must be followed. We cannot believe the biblical vision for the healing of creation and the church's place in this work and stay as we are. There are immediate changes which become necessary to our present ways of living and relating if we are to see their fulfilment. They will not come to pass apart from our response, but through it. For Baptist Christians this means changes in present behaviour and patterns of church life. It means the willingness to question what we are doing and how it is done. It means the recognition that what we are now is not what we should be.

The imaginative forms in which the Bible sets before us the picture of a new world should lead to a release of imagination about the patterns of our life now. Church life as it is currently experienced among Baptist Christians is only one of many creative possibilities open to us. Our horizons are limited by the culture that we have inherited and that we suppose to be the norm. We need to have our vision expanded and to enter into an era of change. How I perceive this change in broad terms will be suggested below. Before we become practical, however, it is necessary to try and express in theological terms the vision which we have already considered.

Developing a theology

My task at the moment is to be a theological teacher. I find that for many people the idea of theology is somewhat intimidating. They imagine that theology is all about abstract theory. They assume that theologians are eccentrics who come out of the ivory tower only to cast doubt on the truth of the Christian faith. Such a caricature was well expressed in the TV programme *Yes, Prime Minister!* when Sir Humphrey Appleby gave as his definition that 'theology is a device for keeping people in the church who no longer believe in God'! There is some truth to the caricature, but not much. Theology is the way we think and talk about God.

As all Christians, supposedly, do talk and think about God, this must mean that we are all theologians. We all have our ways of thinking about God, our connected pattern of ideas about him, that spell out for us what he is like and how he works. This is theology and it fulfils a very important function. Having read the Bible, we draw from it a framework of ideas which then govern, or should govern, our behaviour. This is our way of translating the reality which we see in the Bible into the reality which we face in the present world. It is a way of connecting up the truth of the Bible with the facts of our present life. Because our theology affects the way we live now, and may even determine it, it is of great importance.

Theology has been likened to a map. The world is too big a place for any of us to be present in all of it all of the time. For this reason we need maps that we can see and handle and which give us the big picture. They enable us to conceive of that which would otherwise be unimaginable. They also have a very practical function: they help us to find our way around. With the aid of a map we can go where we wish in the most efficient way. When they are wrong they mislead us and this is wasteful of time and energy, not to say frustrating.

There are many different kinds of maps. Some are very simple, perhaps a hand-drawn line sketch giving directions to a particular place, yet they serve the purpose needed and do their job. Others are highly sophisticated and accurate, such as an Ordnance Survey map, and need to be so if they are to locate very exact places for legal or construction purposes. Theology is like this in that many people have a theological map which is equivalent to a drawing on the back of an envelope. It is a rough sketch of the big picture about God and the world. It also does its job quite adequately, enabling them to find their way about. When a person becomes a

Christian, they are given a brief sketch of God, Christ and the Holy Spirit which is sufficient to help them in the early stages. As they grow in faith, the map is filled out in greater detail as they come to appreciate more fully the size of the new world into which they have entered.

Yet more detailed theological maps are necessary and this requires people to put in a lot of time and effort doing the spiritual equivalent of measuring, calculating, drawing, checking and testing. This is where more disciplined theological study comes in. Not everybody needs to do this, but somebody must do it for the sake of everybody else. This is the task of the theologian. It is done by thinking, writing, arguing, disagreeing and rethinking, all with the intention of gaining as much clarity as possible. As with a faulty map, a faulty theology could land you in a ditch or up a creek!

Another thing about maps is that they change. The basic shape remains the same, but details need to be brought up to date as new roads, bridges and motorways are built. Likewise, the basic framework of our theology may remain the same, but the details change as the world in which we live changes. Things that we did not know about previously come to light and require new thinking and statements. Old insights are rediscovered and are restated for the contemporary world. It is not much good finding your way around the country today using a map from the seventeenth century. But the maps we use now have grown out of the maps of previous generations and even an old map can bring something to light that is not so prominent now as once it was. As we all have a theology, we may as well have a good one that will save us from going too far astray.

It is my hope in this section to express theologically, that is in a series of connected ideas, the meaning for today of the biblical vision already stated. What I have to offer is the theological equivalent of a drawing on the back of an envelope. It is not a highly sophisticated statement but it ought to do the job—that is, be a helpful guide for the present. It is an attempt to spell out the meaning of the vision that is before us in a way which relates it to the actual situation of the church in which we find ourselves. What it offers is guiding principles which affect the way we think about the church of today and indicate how the challenge to change needs to be expressed.

There are five principles which set out what needs to happen to the church, and specifically to Baptist churches, if the vision is to be fulfilled. These are set out in as simple a form as possible to present them as a single package and to aid recall.

Renewal

It is essential in a day when churches have a distinct air of old age that they should experience the renewing work of the Spirit. This is necessary at every level. People need to be renewed in their love for Christ and knowledge of him. Their local church institutions need to share in this renewal. So must the denominational structures which were set up to support and help them. We are all acquainted with the phenomenon of decline. All things have a tendency to decline unless they are infused with a new energy. For Christians, this new energy comes from the Spirit of God. The Spirit of God uses the word of God to reveal the emptiness of our present service. This is painful, yet it is the prelude to renewal. From the brokenness of admitting that things are not as they should be there comes new life.

This note of holy discontent with our lives and our institutions seems to be rarer than it should be. Discontent is present often enough, but not holy discontent. Lack of vision has as its partner in complacency, the belief that things are pretty much all right as they are. The intention of this book is not to be unhelpfully critical but to help to stir up the sense that, as it happens, things are not what they should be and the first step towards improvement is to acknowledge it.

We need to be renewed. There are two dimensions to this. We need to be renewed by the Spirit in the image of Christ, to share with him in living fellowship. We need also to be renewed in our relevance to the community in which we live.

Without spiritual renewal we have nothing to give, since there is no true awareness of being transformed by a power that comes from beyond ourselves. To be able to offer something to the surrounding world, churches must become the places where heaven and earth interact, where the eternal impinges upon space and time.

But if this is to happen in a way which makes an impact, the local church must be accessible to the community in which it is set. Its forms of life and worship must be in an idiom with which a substantial proportion of its surrounding population can begin to identify. We are talking here about culture and about cultural relevance. If, in order to become members of the church, seekers after faith must cross large cultural barriers, they are less likely to do so. Renewal must involve therefore the spiritual renewal of the believer and the cultural renewal of the church. Life and relevance must go together.

It is clear that the wave of spiritual renewal associated with the charismatic movement combines these two elements. The Spirit is at work. His activity involves the breaking down of particular church or chapel cultures which have outlived their time. Because believing people have not been controlled by a forward-looking vision but by a deceptive hanging on and harking back to the past, the renewing work of the Spirit has not always been perceived aright. As in the time of Jesus the old wine-skins of institutional Judaism were unable to contain the new wine of the kingdom, so it is today. Yet now the old wine-skins are not Jewish but 'Christian'. The renewing work of the Spirit still makes for change and such change involves still its fair share of pain.

What I am arguing is that Baptist churches, with all other churches, should be open to the renewing work of the Spirit. It is a call for *glasnost*. This is now the issue as far as renewal is concerned. Previous decades may have debated what is meant by baptism of the Spirit or whether we should speak in tongues. These issues are not dead, but they are only relatively important when compared to the issue of openness. When there is a true openness to the Spirit, it becomes difficult to be satisfied with tight definitions of what he may or may not do. But even those who speak in tongues, or claim certain experiences, can close themselves off from the Spirit by rigid attitudes.

True openness, combined with an eagerness to honour the Holy Spirit as Lord and God with the Father and the Son, is a prelude to the coming of the Spirit in fresh grace and power.

Reformation

This is the second principle that belongs to our suggested theology. The renewing of the church must lead to its reformation. This is the conclusion reached by those who were studying their Bibles with new eyes at the time of the sixteenth-century Reformation. The renewal of their faith led to reformation, in part at least, of the church. Moreover, they stated the key principle that the church should always be being reformed in accordance with the Scriptures. Reformation does not happen once but is a continual process. The plain teaching of Scripture is what controls the reformation of the church, not the whim of fashion or short-lived preference.

In affirming this principle, the Reformers were showing great wisdom. Tradition is very powerful. In the Roman Church, the authority of tradition was such that it obscured the authority of the Bible. Exactly the same tendencies are visible in the churches which emerged from the Reformation. Having established a new tradition, that tradition tended to become an authority in a way which threatened to make the Bible a lesser authority in the church.

The same feature is observable in Baptist churches, although it is not the 'tradition' that is referred to but 'the way we do things', or 'the Baptist way'. Now, clearly, we all have a tradition since all this means is that certain things have been handed on to us. We should be conscious of standing in a tradition because this is honest. But the most important thing that our Baptist forebears have taught us is not to accept anything just because they taught us it. Scripture must judge and we must judge according to Scripture.

The power of tradition is that cultural factors are slowly added to the church until the point comes where they cause a serious distortion of the basic message we proclaim. The unscriptural teachings against which the Reformers protested began life as part of the culture in which the church was living, and gradually were adopted into the mainstream of church life.

Baptist Christians face this same pressure. The cultural factors which have been added to our experience of faith are largely Victorian in nature. The forms of architecture, of music, of institutional life, of church organisation which characterise Baptist Christians of the twentieth century were powerfully shaped by the culture of the Victorian era. These may have been all right at the time and may have aided the cultural relevance of the churches to that era. But they also have their distorting effect. If left unreformed, they assume a power they should not have. What is needed is the work of reformation to alter present reality in favour of scriptural teaching. This reformation will involve both the local church and the denominational structures which have been developed between the churches. There is a further principle however.

Restoration

Here is a word calculated to make the blood of a good denominational Baptist boil, especially if he or she lives in the south of England! The restoration movement is rather con-fusingly regarded in Baptist circles. Sometimes it is referred to, especially by those in denominational organisations, as the 'renewal movement'. This is incorrect. Charismatic renewal is a movement which has touched all denominations. 'Restora-tionism' is a facet of the renewal movement which is operating with the belief that church life needs to undergo a restoration of a particular kind in accordance with Scripture.

The details of this restoration will not here detain us. Because this movement has taken a particularly attractive and well-articulated form in the south of England, many Baptist churches have lost members in large numbers to it. Some have joined it wholesale without jettisoning their official Baptist identity. For some time the movement appeared to Baptists in a very threatening light, although this factor has now diminished considerably. Yet the attraction and challenge of this movement to many has meant that some Baptists have been galvanised into action to give an account of themselves and their own identity.

The paradoxical element in all of this is that Baptists who have felt some distaste for restorationists appear to have lost sight of the fact that they are themselves restorationists. That this can be forgotten is itself an indication that many Baptists have lost touch with their roots. They have begun to see themselves as an established denomination and to accommodate to the styles and attitudes of their counterparts in the established churches against which they were originally a protest. When Baptists criticise restorationists for starting new churches, attracting members and generally being radical, they should remember that they have previously done it all themselves.

The belief that the church needed to be restored according to the New Testament pattern is a fundamental Baptist principle. It differs from the ideas of the mainstream Reformation churches established by Luther and Calvin and from the compromise attempted in the Church of England, in believing that the church as it had been inherited was probably too corrupt to be adequately reformed. What was needed was a return to first principles as revealed in Scripture and a thoroughgoing re-establishing of the churches upon that basis.

The mainstream Reformation was not itself enough, since it left the medieval church virtually intact as a state-controlled organisation using worldly power to enforce its will on people. Both Luther and Calvin argued for such an alliance. The Reformation was therefore only a partially successful attempt to be true to Scripture. A thoroughgoing restitution would have swept away the form of the church as it then existed, in favour of believers' churches practising believers' baptism, with genuine freedom of conscience and free from state control.

It is not perhaps surprising that such radical demands were met with intense fear and that their early proponents were fiercely persecuted, not least by the Reformation churches. These nonconformists were felt to be a grave threat to the order of things. What interests us here is the principle of restoration and its relevance to today. Renewal leads to reform. But to reform what exists is only part of the concern of the Bible-believing Christian. What if there are elements in the biblical testimony which have been lost and forgotten in the course of the centuries? Should not churches concerned to return to their biblical roots be prepared for that which has been lost to be restored, even if for hundreds of years the biblical heritage has been completely lost?

In returning to the apostolic practice of believers' baptism, this is precisely what the early Baptists were doing. We find it difficult to imagine how startling this action was. The principle of restoration is a reminder that the Lord has yet more light and truth to break forth from his word.

It is for this reason that Baptist Christians ought to listen carefully to the voice of the Spirit in charismatic renewal and embrace with conviction what they perceive to be truly of God. To argue that this charismatic renewal is not the Baptist way, that it does not belong to our tradition, is the very pitfall of traditionalism against which we stand. Charismatic renewal is among the contemporary challenges which a reformation and restorationist view of the authority of Scripture poses. It is not the only one and it is not the last. The worst possible attitude that Baptist Christians could adopt towards it is that of distant toleration or of polite but condescending interest. If God is in it, so should we be. It should not be seen as an optional form of spirituality for those who are so inclined, but as an aspect of the total work of God from which we genuinely desire to benefit. For this reason we cannot afford not to embrace whatever there is in it which is of God, nor must we fail to integrate what it offers into our total life.

Revival

The logic of the principles we have so far considered takes us further. Those whose faith arises from the New Testament, and is nourished by it, will be deeply challenged by the testimony it gives to the power of the Spirit of God. The first church came into existence as a direct result of the explosive energy of the Spirit which erupted on the Day of Pentecost. At the very least, this indicates to us that the church of Christ will always find its life in the Holy Spirit, that it cannot exist without him.

But because the Spirit is sovereign and free, and has it within his power to take us by surprise, he will not always act according to the norms we lay down for him. Within his repertoire he has the freedom to work in process and in crisis, in the ordinary and the extraordinary. Much of what we have so far outlined concerning renewal, reformation and restoration can be understood in terms of the gradual, progressive development of the church. The word 'revival', however, takes us into new territory.

In the history of the church there have been significant, intense bursts of the Spirit's work with great creative power and remarkable results in terms of conversions and social impact. The coming of the Spirit at Pentecost was one such occasion. In short moments like this, much is forged. The principle of revival is not one that can be categorised as a programme for the church, because it is inevitably outside its control. The profound sense of our need for God and the comings of his Spirit should, however, be characteristic of every church and every Christian. It is the reminder that the work and mission of the church is not a question of human effort but of divine power.

If there is a vision which inspires us for the future, it is not one which is humanly achievable. The ultimate and penultimate hopes can only come to pass as God himself acts. They are not evolutionary developments but the product of the power of God. One of the great contemporary advocates of hunger for revival was Martyn Lloyd-Jones, with whose words we agree:

> This is no age to advocate restraint; the Church today does not need to be restrained, but to be aroused, to be awakened, to be filled with a spirit of glory, for she is failing in the modern world.

For this reason, the principle of revival is one that we must build into our theology and with which we must reckon.

Reconstruction

This leads us to a final principle to guide us. All we have so far said concerns the church. This is not an embarrassment because the centrality of the church in the plan of God is something in which we believe. But the vision which is guiding us is a vision of God's purpose for all things, and the church must be seen in this light. It is the people-in-community whom God is using in a central role to fulfil his purpose. The church does not therefore exist for itself but for the sake of God's work in the world. That work is a work of reconstruction, of *perestroika*. Its end is the reshaping of all human life in the image of Jesus Christ.

It begins with the reconstruction of individuals and moves on into the reshaping of all human existence. It is guided by a hopeful vision which sees the saving purpose of God finally redeeming all things. At the same time, it is a realistic vision since it recognises that there is resistance to God's initiative on the part of individuals and the powers which determine and shape the world we know. Whatever reconstruction of alienated human society may be achieved now, it must await its completion in God's fulfilment in history, the time of which we do not know.

Yet the coming future of liberation may be anticipated and celebrated in the present by a free people working for the freedom of other people. Whatever enslaves people— whether it is the inner guilt resulting from sin, or the existence without hope or meaning of the many, or the corporate enslavement of whole peoples by unjust systems and social forces—has been, is being and will be overcome in Christ. Those who believe are sharing in God's work to set the people free. This is the work of reconstruction, and it requires our conscious and willing participation to bring it to reality.

The alternative is a religious quietism which fails to follow God in his self-giving involvement in the world. This distorts the church. Only when the church is seen against the horizon of God's love for the world is it seen in its true light. The spiritual *glasnost* with which we began leads us to a social *perestroika*.

In this simple form, outlining five principles, there is a package of ideas which is capable of pointing us ahead. For some, they may seem to be too simple. The fact is that it is simple ideas, with which people can connect, which are more likely to change the world than any others. These principles are able to serve Baptist Christians as an agenda for change. Yet ideas are ideas and many people do not function easily in that world. What is the cash value of such ideas? How may they be applied to the forms of church life which are to be found among Baptists? This is the next topic for investigation.

Making the shifts

My argument is that the biblical and theological work that we have done in this chapter leads to the practical process of renewing and reforming the life of Baptist churches. Change is urgently required. I intend to represent the needed changes in terms of shifts in emphasis and practice. The word 'shift' is not accidental. As we shall see as we progress, we need to shift from where we have been to where we could be without throwing out the baby in the bath water. The words of Jesus about the teacher of the law being like 'the owner of a house who brings out of his storeroom new treasures as well as old' (Mt 13:52) are relevant here. It is wise to know what must change and what must be preserved.

With these cautionary words, we are nevertheless arguing for a new order of church life to emerge. The ground we have already covered indicates that unbridled change is not advocated, but a process of change controlled by the biblical witness and in accordance with Baptist principles most certainly is. What is needed is the emergence of a new order of Baptist churches out of the old order, expressing renewed Baptist identity. What shifts are required to make the transition?

Worship

The first is in the area of worship and I would characterise it as a shift from the *solemn* to the *celebratory*. Now for some time this shift has been underway among all kinds of Christians. It has been fuelled by the charismatic renewal movement, resourced by large numbers of new songs of varying quality, modelled by the new churches which have sprung up outside the system and inspired by Spring Harvest and other such jamborees. The characteristic tension it has produced has been between great enthusiasm on the part of some and antagonism on the part of others who have felt and said, 'The old is better' (Lk 5:39).

It is not surprising that worship should prove such a place of tension, since it occupies a central place in people's lives. It is not spiritual factors alone which come into play here. Musical tastes and preferences can be divisive. There appears to be a musical divide, according as people were formed by a pre- or a post-Beatles culture. We are now living in an age of immense cultural diversity within the one overall culture and it becomes difficult to provide worship which culturally satisfies everybody.

The real challenge, however, is to ask what is the source of our ideas about the nature and form of worship? This is where tradition rears its head once more. For most Baptists, worship has taken a certain form which has come to assume normative status and is tacitly assumed to be the right way to worship. This form combines the use of organ music, hymns from a hymn-book (preferably the *Baptist Church Hymnal* and mainly deriving from the eighteenth and nineteenth centuries); a certain form of architecture involving pews, pulpit and a communion table with chairs; an order of service popularly called 'the hymn sandwich'; and the leadership of one person who would lead the whole service and preach. Add to this combination 'the notices', and we have Baptist worship as it has generally been practised in this century. It will be familiar to most Baptists.

Before commenting on it as a form of worship it must be obvious that it is very much the product of a particular culture at a particular time, namely British culture of the post-Victorian era. This can hardly make a claim to be the norm. What many have failed to recognise is that the form of worship they have espoused is itself a departure from the Baptist tradition.

While the organ has been considered the only appropriate vehicle (the 'anointed instrument') for accompanying worship in church, they forget that previous generations (Spurgeon, for instance) refused to have any instrument in church other than the unaided human voice, and still earlier generations frequently had more varied forms of musical accompaniment. While they bemoan the passing of the hymn, they forget that hymns were an innovation of the eighteenth century, at which time some devout Baptists found anything other than the Psalms difficult to accept. Churches split over the issue. Many felt the inclusion in worship of man-made hymns unacceptable. Some felt that any congregational singing was unspiritual, on the ground that it encouraged non-believers attending services to sing hypocritically (not a weak argument!).

In a similar way, we forget that the 'hymn sandwich' was a product of the Victorian age and was introduced, along with choirs and anthems, to spice up a previous form of worship which had begun to become dull. Likewise, the nonconformist Neo-gothic which was adopted by Baptists in the last century for their church buildings was a departure from the earlier, simpler and smaller meeting houses where they gathered for worship. It is arguable that the newer forms of worship which have begun to develop and the more recent forms of architecture bear more resemblance to Baptist origins than those which have come to be accepted as the norm.

It may well be the case that the chapel culture that we have inherited was appropriate for its day and enabled the churches to be relevant to their environment. But this is no longer the case. Chapel culture must adapt, in form and expression, to the culture that now exists and which is rich in its variety. This can be argued purely on the grounds of the need to be relevant. But there is a more substantial reason for reforming worship, namely, that it is justified biblically.

It is certainly true that any form of worship is dependent upon the sincerity with which it is offered and there are no superior forms of worship because of this. But a respect for biblical patterns of worship leads to the conclusion that many forms of worship are legitimate. This is particularly true of the Old Testament, for although the ritual and sacrifices of the Temple must be seen as fulfilled in Christ and therefore inappropriate in the New Covenant, the Old Testament legitimates the joyful celebration which is being newly discovered.

Psalm 150 envisages the use of many musical instruments in the praise of God. Psalm 149 speaks of singing and dancing, Psalm 47 of clapping hands. Whereas there is no biblical precedent for our familiar 'close your eyes, hands together' approach to prayer, the Old Testament tradition sees prayer taking place with hands and eyes lifted to God (Ps 123:1; 134:2). Such bodily actions speak of openness to the God who is beyond us, whereas closing eyes and clasping hands is the body language of retreat into oneself.

I am not arguing that we must employ these forms of bodily expression in worship, since that would be a false legalism. I am saying that when the power and joy of the Spirit of God begin to break beyond our cultural modes, we must allow the Bible to guide us. Our worship must be related to our culture but when it becomes trapped by our culture, we are in trouble.

The ideas of propriety in worship, of what constitutes 'reverence', which are found among Baptists often have little to do with the Bible or with true spirituality. Rather, they reveal a fear of legitimate emotion and of bodily expression which reflects a religious culture that is less than whole in these respects. The criticism, sometimes voiced, that free worship might become sensual can equally be applied to any activity in worship, including preaching and singing. But beneath it there is also an unresolved fear of the body which is characteristic of the Western religious tradition. A healthier attitude accepts that, as we belong body, soul and spirit to God, our worship should involve the offering of body, soul and spirit in the power of the Holy Spirit.

Our worship, then, needs to shift from the solemnity which has been its hallmark to being a celebration of the love and goodness of God. It should reflect the fact that Christ truly is risen. I recall on one occasion being told that the only kind of joy permitted in church was solemn joy. I have never discovered what this looks like. I imagine that it means joy should be felt deep down but should not be allowed to be expressed overtly in case it becomes exhibitionism, or possibly causes embarrassment. Sometimes I wonder whether the average Baptist would have felt at all comfortable as a member of the early church, which did not appear to have a problem with these things.

Celebratory worship has room for psalms, hymns and spiritual songs; for raised or clapping hands, dancing feet and praising voices; for spiritual gifts and hearty participation; for the use of instruments, drama and the visual arts; and for preaching and teaching. Worship should be an event. Things should happen when God's people gather. It is more than a service which we attend and then go away from unchanged; it is a meeting with God and his family, with a sense of expectancy and thankfulness. It is an occasion which is greater than the sum of its parts because when we gather, the presence of the Lord counts for something and is not just a theory.

This kind of worship is more than an aspiration, because it is already happening in many places and needs to happen all the more if we will permit it. The kind of attitude that stands apart from it, and looks down on it because of its lack of adequate sophistication or liturgical skill, is a form of spiritual snobbishness which wants worship to be an elitist activity rather than the response of ordinary people to God. Jesus was a populist and so should we be.

Now for the baby in the bath water. To shift to a celebratory style of worship ought not to exclude the solemn. A church in which joy is the only permitted emotion would be as unreal as its opposite. Living as we do in a world which is constantly being torn apart and with which the church is joined by a common humanity and the love of Christ, it is essential for the pain of the world to be felt within the congregation of God's people.

There is no reason why this should not be the case in a community which focuses upon the two events of cross and resurrection to gain light on its life. For the believer, the pain of the cross and the joy of resurrection are held together in worship as in life. But finally it is the resurrection which is the last word of God to our condition. Christian worship will certainly be in touch with the suffering of the creation, its groaning and yearning for freedom, but will also express the reality of liberation now for those who are in Christ.

Structures

A second shift is required in the area of church structures, which I describe as a shift from the *organisational* to the *organic*, or from the *institutional* to the *charismatic*. Institutionalisation is the bane of any organisation. Once structures have been established to serve the life of the people, there is an inevitable tendency for those structures to forget the purpose for which they were created and (to use personifying language) to become self-important. This can be observed as a

matter of routine at the local church
easier to start an organisation than to

Once in existence, organisational
arena in which people fulfil their exist
source of identity, meaning and eventual
Having been created to serve, they end up
attracted to themselves a loyalty which
primary loyalty to the church community
this condition is achieved, the church is up-e .... members of the church are press-ganged into the service of the structures. Irrespective of gifting, individuals are recruited to maintain the structures that exist.

This phenomenon may be observed particularly with Sunday Schools and uniformed youth organisations. Both are people-hungry and eat people (which is wrong!). Some churches are operating with an organisational superstructure of committees and departments which is entirely inappropriate to the present size or nature of its membership. It is a relic of a former age which nobody has ever found the energy to change. This is because changing it does in fact take a great deal of energy. The result is that good people are tied up spending themselves in things which are inefficient as far as the kingdom of God is concerned. A shift is necessary.

The shift I have described is away from organisational, institutional forms towards perceiving the church as a charismatic organism. The churches are living organisms composed of people with gifts. The shift of perception involves seeing that their gifts must be identified and the church organised around that which God has equipped them to do. The people involved in youth or children's work should be those who are gifted in these areas. If fewer are so gifted, perhaps this is a sign that the work should be concentrated in some other area. Only in this way can we overcome the frequent phenomenon of churches where a small group does all the work and the rest of the people form a large, passenger fringe. As the church takes account of the gifts which have been bestowed on each, and gives opportunity, the level of involvement is increased.

to go about this is to begin to ask a very significant
: what is the vision God is giving us? Those who are
g gifted by the Spirit will have a sense of vision for what
they are gifted to do. The converse is true. We should not do
what we lack the vision for.

In one church to which I belonged, this principle came to
light in an interesting way. Each year we had been in the habit
of entering a float in the local carnival. We had done it for
years and it belonged to the tradition of the church and the
surrounding community. It was an annual pain in the neck
because nobody really wanted to do it. Yet the institution
demanded that people be pressed into service. One year we
thought to ask the question 'Does anybody have the vision for
this?', with the implication that those who did could do the
work. As it happened, nobody had the vision for continuing
what had been, but there was a vision for using the event as an
evangelistic occasion.

This released new energy, with the result that a successful
enterprise was mounted. After this, each year we asked,
'What do we have the vision for?' Sometimes there was no
vision at all, in which case nothing was done. Mostly there was
vision for varying forms of evangelistic enterprise, which were
well carried through. The point is that where people are
stirred about something, the will to achieve it will be found.
Instead of being constrained by the institution and tradition,
we learned in that church to keep things on a short rein and to
enquire carefully before engaging in any enterprise about
vision and gifting. It made a difference to the way the whole
church functioned and provided a way of making the transition from organisation to organism.

Of course, there is a baby in this bath water as well. The
emphasis on gifts can become a subtle way of opting out of
responsibility. 'It's not my gift' can be a pseudo-spiritual way
of saying 'not on your life!'. It can become a way in which
people do what they want to do and no more. Frankly, there
are times when it is good for people to be constrained by the
organisation, to put themselves out and do something they

would not altogether have chosen. Some things just have to be done and are a matter of service. The theology of gifts therefore needs to be matched by a theology of servanthood. In this mix of emphases there is a healthy form of church life. Nevertheless, the need for Baptist churches in the main is to shift towards a more organic concept and practice of the church.

Government

The third shift concerns the way the churches are governed, and I identify this as a shift from *constitution* to *consensus*. As the subject of church government is addressed in a later chapter, I will not attempt to say everything at this stage but simply to indicate a direction of thought. The question of how the churches are governed (or govern themselves) is a crucial one for Baptist Christians. They have something distinctive to offer in this respect, but they will only be able to do so if they can rescue themselves from a preoccupation with constitutional forms of government and rediscover a sense of what it means to discern the mind of the Lord in fellowship with one another.

Over the years, with the development of the British constitution and the formalising of business procedures, there has been a parallel tendency in Baptist churches to conceive of decision-making along the lines of parliamentary democracy, that is to say, in terms of motions, amendments, voting and majority rule. The result has been distortion. To manipulate the rules and procedures of a meeting does not require spirituality but a certain cast of mind learned by those who know how to play power games. This (power games) is what some church meetings have become. A shift is needed from concern with constitutional methods to consensus, that is, sensing together what the mind of the Lord might be for his church and pursuing this on the basis of common agreement.

The baby in the bath water of this particular proposal is that, for two reasons, it is impossible to do without some kind of constitutional form. One reason has to do with the kind of society in which we live, which requires for legal reasons that some such form be assumed. The second is that constitutions may usefully serve the process of consensus when rightly understood and rightly used. This said, such a shift is vitally important if we are to be true to the New Testament theology and practice of church life. A more extensive justification of this statement will be given in the appropriate place.

Evangelism

A further corrective concerns the evangelism of the local church and is a shift from *programme* to *power* evangelism. I am here self-consciously using the terminology of John Wimber, who argues for an approach to evangelism which relies less on programmes of evangelism, which maximise the organisational element. In its place, he argues for an awareness of the power of the Spirit of God to confirm the preaching of the gospel with signs and wonders. In this, he is reacting against forms of evangelism which risk being impersonal and mechanical in nature. Evangelism should involve person-to-person contact and be assisted by unusual enabling of the Spirit to make the gospel effective.

This is how the first church engaged in the task and achieved remarkable results, without any of the programmes adopted in the Western, specifically North American, world. At the centre of this evangelistic strategy is the local church, a community of ordinary people experiencing extraordinary reality in the Spirit.

For a number of reasons it seems to me that John Wimber is pointing us in the right direction. It is part of the legacy of North American evangelical Christianity to employ techniques of evangelism. Response to the gospel is elicited by techniques which risk becoming manipulative and producing only the appearance of spiritual life. But conversion is the transformation of lives by the power of the Spirit, not the mass-production of stereotypical response. Furthermore, the practice of evangelism, as all other aspects of our lives, needs to be informed and shaped by what we read in the New Testament.

Undoubtedly, much that is done today is questionable in New Testament terms. This does not necessarily invalidate it, since each generation must find ways of presenting the gospel for its time. But reliance on the power of the Spirit to give authority to the message is essential. The model of churches leading spiritually eventful lives and supporting Spirit-led Christians in their spiritually eventful witness, is a good one.

The baby in the bath water for this point must be that, although the power of the Spirit is pre-eminent, unless believers are to move purely in their own circles they must develop programmes of activity that bring them into contact with people they would not otherwise meet. At this point, all the well-tried channels such as door-to-door work, street and open-air witness, concerts, coffee bars and missions come into their own as channels along which the power of the Spirit may flow from church to community.

Mood

I believe that there should be a shift in the dominant mood of church life from the *formal* to the *informal*. Why is this important? A lesser reason would be that this is a shift which has already taken place in society generally and it belongs to the social relevance of the local church to reflect it. This change is noticeable in dress, in speech and in manners. It has to do with the breaking down of social and class taboos and is resulting in a less rigid society. In so far as it reflects a less class-conscious society, it is to be welcomed.

More important, however, is the need to break away from an externalism which judges people on the basis of social conventions. The older standards which decreed that church attendance should go hand in hand with certain clothes and attitudes emphasised the outer appearance rather than inner reality. If the predominant model of church is institution, then it will tend to require formality from those who participate. If it is family, or friendship or community, it will be careless of social conventions and more concerned about reality of relationship.

Thus considered, the style of the church should be obvious. Within the family there will be those who adopt a more formal style for their own dress and behaviour and yet are able to co-exist happily with those for whom informality is more natural. It belongs to the tolerance of family and friendship that all are accepted on the basis, not of social conformity, but of a love which values people for themselves and looks upon the heart. This point would hardly be worth mentioning were it not for the attitudes which are still encountered and which conceive of the kind of behaviour which is appropriate in church in a remarkably narrow way.

The baby in the bath water is that there are times when informality is quite inappropriate to the needs of a given situation. Formal occasions are part of the texture of life because this is the best way to mark certain aspects of life. Yet these can be incorporated within a way of life which is warm-heartedly informal and more concerned that people should be at ease than enclosed in a religious overcoat that encourages neither them nor true religion.

Lifestyle

The final shift which is advocated here is in the area of lifestyle and is from the *conformist* to the *Christian*. It used once to be the case that to follow Jesus Christ as a Baptist Christian automatically meant to take up a position of radical noncon-formity. The alliance of church and state meant that to dissent in matters spiritual was also an act of civil disobedience. It was a refusal to conform to what was felt to be in the interests of an harmonious society—agreement in matters of religion. There are still important issues which need to be discussed in this area and in a later chapter we shall examine what it might mean to be nonconformist today.

Here, we raise the question of whether Baptist Christians are now so conformed to their society that they reflect more the image of the world than of Christ. We underestimate the degree to which we are pressed into the mould and in being conformist, we lose any possibility of presenting to the world an alternative society living by a better code in a higher strength.

Take the issues of racism, sexism, materialism and militarism. These four key issues for our society require a positive witness from the Christian community, and yet the instinctive reaction of many Christians in these areas would probably put them on the side of the reactionary status quo. This in itself is worrying. What is worse, however, is the apparently uncritical way in which many hold their moral, social and political views, without reference to Jesus Christ as the One who determines our whole existence. Different political views in the church of Christ may be understandable and even positive. What is inexcusable is unwillingness to make this area the subject of careful Christian thinking so that we hold our opinions in the light of Christ.

Even worse is the tendency to appropriate the Bible in the service of our group, class or nation (as it is capable of being used) and so to lend divine authority to sectional interests. Anyone who doubts that this happens need only consider the use of Scripture to support South African apartheid or North American nationalism to get the point. Yet what others do in a way we cannot fail to notice, we do ourselves without realising it. Ideologists of left and right are equally prone to read their views into Scripture and then claim it in support. Being aware of this danger, of the spectacles with which we read Scripture and the self-interest which controls us, is crucial if we are to learn how to guard against it.

But in Scripture there is a guide, and we should not be deflected from the desire to learn from it, and above all from Christ, how we should live for him amid the complex issues of our time. This is to be truly Christian, and to be transformed along these lines is the reason for the church's existence.

Together, these shifts constitute a challenge to change from what now is to what could be. It is a call to a new order of church life which will simultaneously bring us closer to the New Testament and to the people of our generation. Between these two poles, of faithfulness to Scripture and relevance to our culture, lies the success of Baptist churches in fulfilling their mission as we move towards the next millennium.

3

The Ideal Church

After the collection of ideas in the last two chapters and before going on to expound them further in those that follow, a change of tempo might be helpful. There are different ways of communicating and one of them is to paint a picture. Sometimes this medium communicates more, to more people, more immediately, than any other method. Now, I am no good at painting so I have to attempt to paint a picture using words. It is a picture of the ideal church.

Everybody tells me this church does not exist and so there is no point thinking about it. My less polite friends tell me not to join it when I find it because I am bound to spoil it. Having heard the joke before, I do not let it put me off. Besides, they have not heard me properly. I said the ideal church, not the perfect church. I know the perfect church does not exist but then I do not really want it to. Like most Christians, I want to belong to a church where I am needed, where the little that I have to offer can be used.

That is where the ideal church comes in. It is ideal because it gets down to the real job of making a difference. To paint the picture of this church requires a flight of fantasy. Whatever might be said about the rest of this book, this chapter will be fantastic! By the end of it, you might think I have gone over the top. On the other hand, it might get you to dream dreams too. Who was it who said, 'Some men look at things as they are and ask, why? I dream of things as they could be and ask, why not?'?

If you know me, and recall that I am an exile in a foreign land, it won't surprise you to know that this ideal church is set in the north of England. Actually, it is near the inner city of a large university town. More than this we need not specify—it could be a number of places. The first thing that strikes us about the church is the meeting place in which they gather. Some years ago, when the church was dying and almost dead, providence intervened in the form of a large supermarket chain. What the church had previously considered a liability of a church building was found to be of considerable value because of its position. Four years previously, a new pastor had moved to the church to try and revive the cause. Here was a marvellous opportunity. The supermarket chain was prepared to build a new suite of premises on a strategic site a quarter of a mile away.

As it happened, the pastor had been putting to the church the possibility of selling up and doing without a building, or purchasing a small shop as a worship centre. The possibilities for mission in this new situation were endless. The church had spent much time discussing what kind of a building they ought to erect and what were the principles involved. They had emerged from their discussions with certain clear ideas.

First, the new worship centre should not look like a religious building but should be warm and attractive in appearance. Secondly, it should be a flexible building and even the worship area would be flexible in layout, avoiding any ecclesiastical style that was likely to become outdated. It should also be capable of being renovated at minimal cost.

Eventually the architect had drawn up plans for what looked at first glance like a high tech warehouse with windows. Outside there was ample carparking space. Inside, a large foyer opened up into a large, carpeted hall big enough to contain up to 500 people when various side rooms were incorporated by removing partitions. As we shall return to the worship area, a quick visit to the rest of the building is in order.

The suite is excellently provided for in terms of offices and small meeting rooms. The permanent members of staff each have their own rooms and there is an administration area containing typewriters, word processors, photocopiers and the like. Having cash available from the sale of the old premises, the church took the attitude that it was going to have an excellent system of administration and had set out to do this. Elsewhere on the premises was a sports hall, marked out for various activities. Above the hall, a whole collection of smaller rooms provided for all kinds of group activities. On the ground floor the kitchens were laid out next to a coffee bar/restaurant able to cope with up to 100 people.

The impression conveyed by the premises is functional rather than ornate, but this is prevented from becoming impersonal by the layout of the rooms and the warm and welcoming effect of the whole. So here is a church which has an excellent set of premises. But what about the people?

We arrive at the buildings in time for the Sunday morning gathering. The place is already a hive of activity and people are busy preparing for worship. At the door, a man and a woman are serving as stewards and are welcoming people warmly with handshakes and, occasionally, hugs or kisses. Beyond them are other stewards directing people into the worship area. As visitors, we receive a warm welcome, but it is not overdone. The attitude is friendly and open.

As the people settle down or go about their activities, we are able to weigh them up. About 200 people are gathering. They come in all shapes and sizes, span the age range and are variously dressed. Some are attired in suits or jackets, others in jeans and tee-shirts. It is not easy to tell what social groups they come from but it is immediately obvious that this is a multi-racial congregation. Black and brown faces are strongly in evidence but there are also folk of oriental origin and quite a number who do not fit easily into any racial group. As we await the start of the meeting for worship, the people are already meeting with each other, mingling, sharing news. Some are standing outside in the coffee room drinking tea or coffee. There is a fair level of noise but nobody seems to bother. Several people engage us in conversation and find out who we are and why we are there. There is a sense of expectation in the air.

Then, about five minutes before the advertised time of worship, a group of musicians begins to play. People take their places and begin to settle down. Four or five people, casually but neatly dressed, take their seats at the front. Worship is about to begin.

As we listen to the music, we have opportunity to savour the surroundings. The room could obviously hold a lot more people but is set out with chairs for about 250, most of which are filled. Families are sitting together. The chairs have been arranged sideways-on in a large semicircle, with plenty of space between the rows and at the sides. At the front there is a slightly raised platform where people we assume to be the leaders are sitting. To their left is a group of musicians. At the moment, only a pianist is playing but in addition we can see a guitarist, a bass guitarist and various wind instruments, including a saxophone. The pianist is being joined now by another keyboard which sounds like a synthesiser.

As they play, the congregation begins quite spontaneously to sing and it is obvious that they both love to sing and know how to do it. The room is filled with harmony. Immediately in front of us, we now notice a large screen above the low platform. The words of a song appear on it. We later learn that this is a television screen and that, because of the technological wizardry now available, it is possible to screen the words of any song and virtually anything else. This means the congregation is able to draw upon whatever music it wishes to enrich its worship. I do not know what the copyright implications are, but assume that someone has investigated this and come to some agreement. It certainly works very well.

Nobody is encumbered by any books and everybody must look up!

The song is now coming to a close and a woman on the platform gets up and briefly welcomes people to the church. A few words from the Scriptures and a simple prayer lead into a series of songs of thanksgiving. The same full-voiced singing rings out. The harmonies give a depth to the music that surprises us, almost as if people have taken lessons in how to sing. We later find out that congregational singing is taken very seriously and that from time to time attention is given to drawing out the singing abilities of the people. It is obvious that the people like to worship. The songs of thanksgiving appear to be parts of the Psalms put to music and are accompanied by some clapping, by hands raised in the air and faces lifted towards heaven. The mood of praise lasts for over fifteen minutes during which some people can be observed dancing, some of them in ways full of artistic expression, others simply in joy.

All of this appears to be perfectly normal. Some of the older folks appear quite content to sit down as the praise continues. After twenty minutes, the music subsides and several people, men and women, speak prayers of praise from the floor. When this is done, the woman who is (apparently) leading from the platform invites people to sit down and indicates that the children present may leave for another place. While this is happening, the musicians play and once the exodus has been completed a man comes to the microphone, repeats the welcome given at the beginning and shares some brief items of news. As he does this, the television screen shows various activities that are taking place in the week. Before he steps down, various other people stand up from the congregation to share items of news and concern.

This done, the man at the microphone leads in a prayer lifting to God the various things mentioned and then offering to God with thanksgiving the gifts that are about to be made. As he steps down, baskets are passed along the rows for people to make their offerings. At this point the mood of the meeting changes slightly.

Having resumed her position at the front, the worship leader is introducing several songs which serve as an introduction to a quiet and reflective time in which there is a deep sense of the presence of God. The silence lasts for several minutes and concludes as people from all parts of the room pray, prophesy, speak in tongues and interpret, or lead the gathering in further songs of worship. A general theme joins all these contributions together and is commented on by the worship leader as she draws the whole to a close and then announces the singing of a well-known hymn.

When this has been sung, a man whom we assume to be the pastoral leader takes his position at the front and opens the Bible. Readings from the Old and New Testaments prepare the way for a simple, clear and well prepared explanation of the passage set for study that day. As the exposition progresses, the points that are being made appear on the screen. The preaching is warm-hearted, vigorous, humorous and related to life. It is clearly appreciated by the people, who take careful notes and indicate by their response that the points are not being lost. After half an hour, the preaching ends and the people are invited to stand.

For several minutes the church joins together in carefully prepared intercession for the surrounding community, the needs of the city and current matters of international concern. The people are enabled to participate by means of responses which seem to be part of their regular vocabulary of worship. The prayers are drawn to a close with the Lord's Prayer and the gathering closes with a final song and the grace. The whole thing has lasted for one and a half hours.

Nobody seems in a hurry to leave. We are invited to drink coffee, and find out that the majority of the congregation stays on for a simple lunch once a month, and today is the day. This gives us opportunity to ask further questions. We discover that before the gathering for worship most folk had already attended Christian education classes for the whole age range.

These lasted for forty-five minutes and the current programme for adults was covering such topics as Old Testament
theology, the doctrine of the Atonement, Reformation history and contemporary issues. These were in addition to the
regular groups preparing people for baptism or church membership.

Because of the heavy demands made on church members
on Sunday mornings, the decision had been made to adopt a
more flexible approach to Sunday evenings. In place of the old
evening service, Sunday evenings were now being used for
special interest meetings involving different sections of the
church (men, women, singles, married couples, divorced folk
etc) with a heavy commitment to learning and prayer. This
was in parallel with a regular young people's group which was
proving singularly attractive to outsiders.

On the first Friday of every month without fail, an evening
celebration was held involving the whole church. This was
proving to be the focus of much faith and expectation, and
each month there was a sense of something being achieved on
these occasions beyond the regular rhythm of church life.
These occasions were also important meeting grounds with
those from other churches. All in all, it was felt that the
pattern of meetings provided both a regular discipline of
corporate worship and opportunity for variety. Everybody
appreciated the fact that every effort was made not to over-
burden the church with excessive meetings.

It was interesting also to hear about other aspects of the
church's worship. Communion was celebrated once a month
on Sundays and at least once a month in housegroups or in the
celebration or mid-week gathering. The more recent nonconformist practice of serving the wine in small individual glasses
had been abandoned in favour of a return to the older Baptist
practice of the common cup. When Communion was celebrated, the chairs would be arranged in a circle with a simple
table in the midst bearing a loaf and a dozen well-designed
cups.

The mood of Communion varied. Sometimes, the focus

would be on Christ's atoning work, and a mood of thoughtful and contrite reflection was appropriate. At other times, the focus would be on the risen Lord or the future banquet in the kingdom of God, and joyful anticipation would predominate. By now people had become used to the idea of a common cup. Debates had taken place about whether or not it was hygienic and these had surfaced again once the AIDS problem became known. Medical people in the church had assured the others that fears were groundless, but out of consideration for their concerns care was taken in wiping the cups after use. By now it was felt that the return to the older method added to the symbolism of the occasion and was closer to the biblical practice.

Sunday worship frequently included the presentation of newborn children and this was taken with great seriousness. In discussing baptism, the church had come to a clear mind about the need to welcome children and to affirm their place within the worshipping community. From the attitude of Jesus to children, the church had come to reject decisively the theology which questioned their status in the kingdom of God and consigned them to hell or limbo in the event of an early death. The love of God, not just for the children of the church, but for all children, was emphasised.

At the same time, because of the nature of discipleship, it had been understood that it was neither scriptural nor theologically sound to baptise children irrespective of their own response to the grace of God. Although this was earnestly prayed for and worked towards, it was clearly understood that the child's own responsible decision was crucial at this point. All of this had led to a re-appreciation of the importance of what has been called 'the dedication of parents and the blessing of children' as part of the church's celebration of the gift of life. In the case of believing parents the celebration involved a renewal of commitment on their part to Christian discipleship, and prayer by the church for blessing on the child.

From time to time, parents who had not yet come to faith also brought their children in this way but were not encouraged to make commitments that they could not at this point genuinely sustain. Nevertheless, the church was glad of the opportunity to pray with them and for the child at this important time of their lives. The openness and integrity of the church at this point had led a number of such parents to faith on their own account. The gift of each child was celebrated with the child's introduction to members of the church family who would do their best to care for it in the pilgrimage of life.

A regular highlight of the church's life came round with the baptism of believers. Most months saw baptisms, but not always in the same format. Sometimes special Sunday evening meetings would be arranged to baptise and explain the meaning of faith. Sometimes the baptisms would be part of the monthly celebrations or of the regular family services in which the meaning of baptism could be explained to the whole church family. Always, important seasons of the Christian year such as Christmas, Easter and Pentecost would include baptisms. Baptisms were seen as occasions for the church to celebrate its faith and as important opportunities to bear witness to the gospel.

For this reason, when large numbers of candidates accumulated, the church would sometimes hire part of the local swimming-pool in order to take the witness outside its own premises. Happily, sufficient numbers were coming to believe to make experimentation possible. It had come to be the practice of the church to baptise and then, once the candidates were dried and back among the people, to pray with the laying on of hands that the baptism in water might be a sign of an outpouring of spiritual power upon each candidate. Many were able to bear witness to the fact of a new experience of the Spirit's power because of this. Sometimes there would be visible evidence of this power, with individuals trembling or falling as a result. All of these experiences were treated as the kind of thing that might sometimes happen when the Spirit comes. The worshipping life of this community certainly appeared to be eventful and full of life.

By this time, we had finished lunch and someone suggested

that we might want to meet some of the full-time workers in the church. We were introduced to the pastoral leader who had spoken that morning and he explained the set-up and some of the values of the church. The church currently had around 180 members, the vast majority of whom had joined the church in recent years, mostly as new believers. A new surge of growth was currently being anticipated.

The policy of the church was not to rush people into membership and as far as possible not to treat church members any differently from non-members. Having said this, it was also expected that no one would assume any important role in the church who was not a member. Although membership was highly regarded, it had also been understood that of first importance was the quality of friendship and commitment between people. This kind of membership was what really counted and formal membership was seen as a helpful way of reflecting and strengthening relationships between people. For this reason it was regarded as essential for people to become a part of the church community and begin to feel at home, before encouraging them to apply for formal membership.

New converts would be baptised as soon as possible after their conversion, baptism being regarded as part of their initiation into Christ. In the course of their preparation, they would be taught the importance and the place of the local church and the need to belong. Baptismal preparation would then be followed by instruction about membership of the church. Unlike some churches, this church had not opted to make baptism conditional on the willingness to enter into formal church membership, feeling that this required a level of understanding which demanded too much at this stage. Instead, new believers were steadily led on in the teaching programme and were encouraged to be baptised and then to become church members as their understanding grew. The system was working well.

They had decided to introduce a degree of discretion about the absolute necessity of being baptised before joining the church as a member. Because a number of people who were part of the church community, and had been believers for many years, had asked if they could join the church as members, it was decided that where such people believed in good conscience that their infant baptism was true baptism, this should be respected. This decision had been arrived at, after much discussion, on the basis that baptism should not be made a legalistic condition of membership. On the other hand, where people did not appear to be acting on conscientious grounds but to be avoiding the challenge of baptism, the church was firm in its insistence on believers' baptism.

In this way they were seeking to be true to the need for baptism of believers and yet to be open to the sensitivities of conscience. By far the majority of people had no difficulty in seeing the need for baptism simply from Scripture.

Because the church membership took seriously the responsibility of giving and gave proportionately from their income, the church was able to support a number of staff-members. Most church members committed voluntarily a tenth of their income to the church. Some whose income was higher than most gave a greater proportion on the 'graduated tithe' principle.

It had been considered vital to set people aside for full-time work and to recognise both men and women, including those from ethnic minorities, in the team. The pastoral leader had been well trained on a traditional pattern of theological education. He was joined by a full-time woman administrator of Asian origin who had previously worked in local government, by a full-time male evangelist and youth worker of Afro-Caribbean origin who had trained as a social worker, and by a white woman pastoral worker who was qualified in general and psychiatric nursing. Both the evangelist and the pastoral worker had also been encouraged by the church to further their training and were pursuing church-based patterns of theological education in connection with a Theological College, with a view to denominational accreditation.

This team was joined by other voluntary workers in the

office and in pastoral care. The husband of the full-time administrator had a well paid job and as part of their commitment to the church she returned half of her salary. Each of the full-time workers had a clearly defined area of responsibility and job description and was expected to work efficiently and responsibly. The pastoral leader was expected to supervise the work of each person as a prime responsibility. Each week the team gathered for planning and prayer on a Tuesday morning and had lunch together. They were bound together in loyalty and trust and enjoyed working together.

In addition, they all served as part of the eldership team which included five other men and women all of whom were in full- or part-time employment, with the exception of one who had taken early retirement. The elders met most Tuesday evenings for prayer and consultation. The decision had been made some years previously to replace the old diaconate with an eldership to emphasise the responsibility of spiritual oversight. The decision had not been regretted; all the elders were liked and respected by the people and provided a variety of role models and a secure core to the church. Out of their fellowship together came a sense of optimism and well-being. They were renowned for their ability to keep confidences and deal honourably with people.

The pastoral leader went on to tell us about the church's sense of mission. Of the regular income, forty per cent was devoted to the service of the church and community outside the local church. Much of this went to three missionary families and other individuals serving overseas. Some of the rest was used in local mission which was thought of in three ways: evangelism, social action and political action.

In evangelism, the church's policy was to use all possible means to bring people to individual commitment to Christ. This included making people aware of the existence of the church through appropriate advertising and leaflet distribution. Door-to-door visitation was regularly carried out as a way of making contact with local people. All of the full-time workers spent some time each week in this work, with the result that the church was becoming well-acquainted with local needs and was regarded by some as the local parish church. The evangelist had made a careful study of the community and had identified several areas of opportunity and need.

One result of this was the use of Sunday evenings for youth-orientated evangelistic work. A remarkable openness was being discovered among the young people of the district. A very fruitful form of evangelism was being used in a locally adapted version of 'Good News Down Your Street'. It had been discerned that most people in the area had little understanding of the basics of the Christian message and the level of interest in hearing it explained one-to-one was relatively high. The area was being covered systematically with letters offering basic instruction, with no obligation or strings attached. Many who went through the initial course were carrying on to further levels and coming to faith.

These opportunities for learning allied to the positive witness of individuals within the community and the vibrant life of the church, were creating a powerful evangelistic mixture. It was expected that conversions would take place. Because of the nature of the area in which the church was set, church members were being asked to develop special interests in evangelism. There were plans for groups of three or four to seek to understand and dialogue with other religious groups, from Jehovah's Witnesses to Sikhs and Muslims. A pattern of 'confessional dialogue' was being thought through which, without lessening conviction, would seek to relate to other religious groups on the basis of mutual understanding, not confrontation. The results so far had been challenging but had begun to clarify issues.

The evangelism of the church was inseparable from its social action. A number of church families had moved into properties in the vicinity of the worship centre and renovated them. Some of these had felt the call to practise some kind of community or extended family living and had sought advice as to how this might best be done. An area of the town which had previously been deteriorating was starting to show signs of a renaissance. It was church policy to have regular working days in the locality when litter would be cleared from the streets and alleys. The local council was providing the necessary tools and equipment and local residents were getting on the bandwagon and joining in the refreshments afterwards.

The church had resolved as far as possible to have a church member in each of the local schools, doctors' and dentists' surgeries and in every local organisation it could identify and legitimately join. Occasionally, evenings of prayer would be devoted to sharing local news and progress. A group had been established to receive and monitor requests for the use of church premises. This sometimes involved research into what organisations stood for. The church buildings had become host to varying activities, on the basis that they served the well-being of the community. In place of a system of rentals the church invited the organisations to make donations towards the upkeep of the buildings and to cover the cost of using the premises. By and large this policy was working well.

The pastoral team hosted occasional meetings of religious leaders for the purpose of mutual understanding. As a result of the research into local needs, parts of the premises had been turned into furniture and clothes stores and regular distributions were made throughout the area. In addition, on two days a week, the church itself ran a luncheon club and meals-on-wheels service for local elderly folk. Through its visitation programme it attempted to visit the elderly in the locality.

In its political action the church had understood that the social conditions of the neighbourhood were directly affected by the policies of local and national government. It had also understood that most issues are complex in nature and need a lot of thinking through. Politically-minded and involved church members were invited to form a think-tank to address specific issues and come to a common mind.

Faced with this task, a consensus emerged as to how the needs of the area might be tackled. Local councillors and MPs had been invited on different occasions to visit the church and answer questions. Faced with a community of well-informed and thoughtful people they had found the experience a gruelling one. This had gained a new respect for the church, and the pastoral staff were now frequently consulted on local matters. Some pastoral opportunities had developed and one councillor was now attending church. One church member had been elected to the council and all mainline political parties in the area were finding a growing Christian presence in their ranks and meetings. Meanwhile, a study group in the church was working on a Christian approach to local politics that could form a consensus for church members involved in different parties.

At this point the pastoral leader decides that he ought to go home and put his feet up. After the programme he has described to us, we tend to agree with him. Happily, his colleague, the pastoral worker, is to hand and is able to help us with our enquiries. We are keen to know how the church's decision-making process works. She smiles as if the question would take a lot of answering. During the course of our conversation we learn that, in the early days of the church's revitalisation, many of the necessary changes, including the sale of the old building, had been opposed by a small minority in the church meeting. This had been a painful time but the caring and patient endurance of the pastor had won agreement to the change.

In the upheavals that attended the move, much teaching had been devoted to the nature of the church as a discerning community, out of which several initiatives had emerged. One was the development of a new attitude of trust on the part of the church, in which a new appreciation was gained of the responsibility of leaders to give strategic leadership. Once an eldership was formed it was felt that there was a strength of wisdom in a number of counsellors.

A further initiative was taken by which the elders would regularly share their dreams and visions with the people without any intention of proposing courses of action or decisions.

These became known as 'off the record briefings' and were intended to give people access to the basic thinking of the eldership well before any specific plans were proposed in any area.

A third initiative was the commitment of the church to learn and study how to make decisions in a godly fashion. This led to a series of guidelines for decision-making which the church set itself and which it described as 'mutual consent'. It involved a recognition on the part of the church of the need to learn how to make decisions and a commitment to do so, as well as the outlining of some guidelines on how issues might be presented, absorbed and decided upon by the church over a given period of time. We asked for copies of this paper for future reference. It sounded interesting.

There were further questions we wanted to ask. How, for instance, did the church relate to other churches and particularly to other Baptist churches? At this point the church had had its own pilgrimage of moving from a position of fierce independency to one of general apathy about other churches and then to one of sensing its responsibility.

On the wider ecumenical front the church had become aware of the common heritage of those who are in Christ and had begun to relate positively and humbly to churches from other traditions. This was expressed partly through the full-time staff in their gatherings with other Christian leaders, partly through a policy of occasionally visiting other congregations en bloc on Sunday evenings, partly through a mid-week series of faith-sharing meetings which had been held in the various churches and partly through co-operation in joint social and evangelistic opportunities. Church members had been surprised at the depth of faith and commitment expressed in other traditions. Concurrently they had been confirmed in their own identity and convictions. Contact with other Baptist churches developed along with the increasing self-confidence of the church.

As it became clear that a good work was taking place, it seemed to be the right thing to share it. A natural channel for this was the existing association network to which the church belonged. The pastoral leaders began to feel a sense of responsibility to participate more fully in the life of the association and resumed regular attendance at meetings. At first the going was tough and bureaucratic but gradually it became possible to change the agenda and feel that a useful direction was being set. A series of progressive appointments to full-time tasks within the association (including an evangelist and church-planter) had transformed the situation and opened up a host of new possibilities.

The churches were beginning to see that much could be done together which would never be done apart. All this seemed to justify the strategic decision to become involved and made the commitment of more time and energy seem worthwhile and productive. The association was becoming a means of contact along which the undoubted energy of this revitalised church could be channelled.

Time is running short and before long we will have to be going. Our interest returns to the people of the church. What makes them tick and what sustains them in their witness? It has already become clear to us that the church is by no means a problem-free zone. The outward buoyancy is not the whole story. Every individual represents a different pilgrimage of faith that has meant passing through pain and sometimes learning to live with it. We learn that the church has developed a particular ministry to the divorced and is in the reconstruction business for broken families. Not every person or family they have sought to help has been a success story. With some folk the church has learned simply to muddle through pastorally, lacking final solutions to their problems.

People get sick and die in this church just like any other and they have learned to rejoice with those who experience healing and to share the pain of those who do not. The church contains the depressed, the abused, the fearful, the bereaved, the doubting. Yet the philosophy has emerged that it is not having problems which we should worry about, but how we deal with the problems we have. The pastoral worker helps us here. Certain values have emerged in the church's pilgrimage which have been identified as crucial in sustaining the spiritual life of the people.

The centrality of Jesus as the One who is to be followed is the most important of these. Love for and service of Jesus of Nazareth is the touchstone by which all other things are measured. Faith is not directed to religion or church but to Jesus as the One whom we are called to obey in life and in death. With this goes a commitment to the orthodox faith of the Christian church as a true interpretation of the manner of God's presence in this man Jesus. Attempts to reduce this understanding are not to be regarded as improvements, but the very opposite. A commitment is embraced to the knowledge of God as the living God, as one who is not just spoken of in B minor but known in experience in the here and now, who affects our existence.

With this goes the belief that the truth of God is to be pondered and thought through continually if life is to be directed aright and that this must be done by oneself in prayer and study as well as together. Encompassing all is the conviction that God's love is for the world and not just the church and that the church has been chosen not for privilege but for responsible living, to work for the transformation of the whole of human life. This prevents the church from becoming closed in upon itself and causes it to be broad in its sympathies, open-minded in its thinking and warm-hearted in its concerns.

These are the values and convictions which have shaped this church. It is clear that the community life of these people is a source of immense strength to them. The fulfilling worship, the warm fellowship, the commitment to teach, learn and serve together all contribute to the creation of a supportive and challenging community such as is desperately needed.

The people of this community very clearly value their life together and are therefore glad to meet. They manage to do this on Sundays as has been described. Wednesdays find them together in housegroups, alternating weekly with central gatherings of the whole church. In order to keep them from going stale, the housegroups are kept on a short rein so that they remain purposeful gatherings. Often, on Wednesday nights together, the agenda is simply prayer but times of prayer can move swiftly into times when important decisions are considered and discussed. These people are not afraid to wrestle with important issues of Christian life and witness.

But they also know that the life of the church is meant to enable them to live as believers in their families and in the community. Relatively speaking, therefore, only a small part of their lives is spent in church—the bulk of it is spent serving the Lord in the community at large. This is the kind of church to which it would be good to belong.

Now that our brief visit is over, I realise that in this last sentence I am speaking for myself. For some, the picture of church life I paint might seem too threatening or too intense. Some prefer their religion quiet and unobtrusive. I make no excuse for not standing with them. At root, no doubt, we might find very different perceptions about what it means to be the church. I would certainly want to argue that my kind of church bears more than a passing resemblance to the first church which met in Jerusalem and of which it is recorded:

> Those who received his message were baptised, and about three thousand were added to their number that day. They devoted themselves to the apostles' teaching and to the fellowship, to the breaking of bread and to prayer. Everyone was filled with awe, and many wonders and miraculous signs were done by the apostles. All the believers were together and had everything in common. Selling their possessions and goods, they gave to anyone as he had need. Every day they continued to meet together in the temple courts. They broke bread in their homes and ate together with glad and sincere hearts, praising God and enjoying the favour of all the people. And the Lord added to their number daily those who were being saved (Acts 2:41–47).

In their own way these words are intended to present us with a picture of an ideal church. Many of the details of what I have described may be related to the picture drawn of the first church or legitimately deduced from it, granted the differences of time and culture.

As it happens, the picture I have attempted to draw is not so imaginary as might be thought. Rather, it is a drawing together of images from many churches of my acquaintance. Not all the aspects are found in one church but are scattered among many. What I describe is a realisable reality and there is every reason why, in the grace of God, churches which parallel this, and others which express an equally vital existence in very different ways, may be found in all places.

4

The Centre of Gravity

In this book we are concerned with the future of Baptist churches and with what has come to be called in recent times, not unhelpfully, 'Baptist identity'. I am seeking to argue that there is hope and great opportunity for Baptist churches and that one of the keys to progress is the recovery and contemporary re-expression of the distinctive values and doctrines which belong to our story.

Identity in the case of human beings has to do, we are told, with genes and especially with particular combinations of genes in the body of each individual. It is this combination which makes for the uniqueness of each person. So it is with Baptist Christians and, in different ways, with any others. It is a number of features coming together that create distinctive identity. Now this needs to be said since even Baptists sometimes imagine that what makes us different is our commitment to believers' baptism. This is certainly the most readily obvious characteristic and the most easily understood and appreciated by others.

However, a moment's thought is enough to show that it is not the whole story. Many others baptise only believers, including the Christian Brethren and the Pentecostals, but they do not regard themselves as being Baptist in the way we are discussing in this book. Similarly, other Christian groups readily affirm doctrines such as the priesthood of all believers, the believers' church and the congregational understanding of church government, without feeling that they are Baptists. What defines the Baptist body is a combination of these particular teachings and values which produces a distinct identity. They are the genes in the Baptist make-up.

This chapter is concerned with an issue which is so crucial that I am entitling it 'The Centre of Gravity'. What we are about to consider is the way the church is governed. There are various terms we can use to describe what is at stake. Often reference is made to 'the congregational order of the church', meaning an understanding of the church which sees the final authority in a church (under Christ as Head) being located in the local church as a whole rather than in either a leadership group in the church or an external authority outside it.

This order is distinguished from episcopalianism (such as in the Roman Church or the Church of England) which locates authority externally in the bishop and internally in his accredited representative (the priest). It is different from presbyterianism (as in the Church of Scotland and many of the new churches) which locates authority in a corporate body of elders in the local church and a synod of elders in the wider church. It also differs from connexionalism (as in the Methodist Church) which locates authority externally in a central ruling body of a national grouping of churches and internally in ministers duly appointed and accredited by such a body.

All of these forms believe, of course, that Christ is the final authority but that his will is mediated to the church through the human means that I have just described.

In distinction from these forms, congregationalism argues that each church must be self-governing and directing. A further way of describing this centres on the role of the church meeting. The congregation is empowered to direct its affairs when it comes together in the church meeting. Here, the congregational concept takes an institutional form. A specific meeting is believed to be the time and place where governmental decisions can be enacted. Most Baptist churches take seriously the need to do things 'decently and in order' and therefore invest the church meeting with an air of formality. A third way of describing this concept is as 'the gathered church' and this, I hold, is the preferable mode of description because it contains a direct allusion to the words of Jesus, which should be seen as crucial, in Matthew 18:19–20:

> Again, I tell you that if two of you on earth agree about anything you ask for, it will be done for you by my Father in heaven. For where two or three come together in my name, there am I with them.

Because these words are so central we shall return to look at them in more detail. For the moment it is enough to notice that when the church gathers in the name of Christ it possesses an authority of agreement before God because of Christ's presence. At the very least, we can say that there is something here we must come to terms with in our understanding of the church. In this chapter the concepts of the congregational order of the church (or just congregationalism), the church meeting and of the gathered church will be used more or less interchangeably.

Here we revisit Baptist history. It belongs to the genius of the early Anabaptists and Baptists that they saw something in their reading of the Bible, in the light of their times, which was of enduring importance. It was negative and positive in nature.

Negatively, they understood that there was a limit to human authority. The religious and political establishments were telling them that they could not obey what they saw in the Bible. The Roman Catholics were telling them that only the Pope could interpret Scripture and that they should submit to his authority. The fledgling Reformed Church under Zwingli was telling them, or so they understood it, that they could only be obedient to certain aspects of Scripture when the town council gave them permission. Thus they felt themselves constrained to act independently on the basis of Scripture and the leading of the Spirit, in defiance of established authority. The authority of God and of conscience was deemed to outweigh that of church and state. 'We must obey God rather than men' (Acts 5:29). Out of small acorns mighty oaks do grow. Out of this act of civil disobedience much has come. Small though it seems, a mighty principle is contained here, namely that there is a limit to what church and state are entitled to require. They have no authority to overrule the authority of conscience in matters of religion. This was a revolutionary principle because it denied the absolute authority of the state.

The congregational order of the church is a development of this. As individuals must be left free to determine themselves in matters of religion, so churches must be left free from political or religious compulsion to determine their own destiny—they must be self-governing. Any religious faith which is imposed or compelled is not genuine. To be free, it must be voluntary. We can see how this developed into belief in baptism as a voluntary act, in churches composed of voluntary members and in the idea that churches should be allowed freedom in matters of religion to determine themselves. This approach to church life works from the bottom up rather than from the top down and marked a radical shift of perception.

The concept of the church meeting served not so much to proclaim that the church was a democratic institution as that it was emphatically not to be dictated to, either by popes, bishops or town councils from without or authoritarian elders from within. It is all about having been set free by Christ for freedom and therefore not submitting again to a yoke of slavery (Gal 5:1).

It is tempting to dwell here for a time and to make two further points. It is mistaken to imagine that what the early Baptists understood was a complete novelty. Others in the history of the church and at the time of the Reformation had moved in the same direction. Similar trends were in motion in society generally. The Baptists were riding an incoming wave, but they were doing more than respond to the spirit of the age. They were recapturing the spirit of early Christianity which had been suppressed by centuries of corrupted church life. They were part of a restoration of New Testament Christianity.

What they rediscovered was in tune with the teaching of Jesus and the apostles, who themselves were at odds with the power systems of their day and were following the ways of God in defiance of them. Jesus was crucified by the religious and civil establishments and rose from the dead in a supreme act of civil disobedience. He just would not fit in and conform. But his dissent has opened the door of liberty for us all.

This brings us to a second point. In asserting the limits of the state, the early Baptists and others like them became the seedbed out of which the freedoms of the Western world have grown. It is not accidental that where nonconformity has been at its strongest, the drive towards democratic societies has been greatest. Democracy has to do with recognising the limits of state control. It conceives of the state as the organ which should protect and enhance the freedoms of the people.

The first Baptist church on English soil was founded in Spitalfields in 1612 by Thomas Helwys, who in the same year published his book *A Short Declaration of the Mystery of Iniquity*. The book was the first demand in England for universal religious liberty and freedom of conscience for all, and led to Helwys being thrown into prison. By 1616 he had died, but others took up the torch and would eventually win the day.

To mark this point is important, because it indicates how God works. Through the church, inklings of the kingdom of God are awakened by the Spirit and grasped firmly by the people. The full implications of those inklings may not be understood, but when faithfully adhered to they become spurs to society as a whole to move towards the new world of freedom from oppression which we call the kingdom of God. Because the faithful church is God's community, it can be the means whereby transforming influences are released in the world. The liberties we currently enjoy are an example of this.

But we should remember that they were dearly bought by the sufferings of our forebears.

So much for the negative significance of the concept of church government with which we are dealing. It turns out not to be negative after all! *Positively* there is much more to add. The early Baptists saw the church meeting/congregational concept as embodying principles of the church which were biblically inescapable, particularly the idea of the priesthood of all believers, which, as we have seen, affirmed the access of every believer to God and the consequent authority of all who believed. They were not simply reacting against certain negative aspects of their culture and developing an appropriate theology to justify their reaction. No doubt they were doing this too (we all do it in different ways) but they were also seeking to live according to positive principles concerning the order of the church, to which they were led by their study of the New Testament. In a moment we shall examine these in some detail.

I began this chapter by claiming that the congregational order of the local church is the centre of gravity for Baptist identity. It is the addition of this element to the mixture that produces the Baptist concoction. At another time and in another place it might be otherwise, but the element of Baptist identity which is contested most today is church government.

When it comes to believers' baptism, it is recognised that there is a strong case. Those who adhere to infant baptism and believe it to be theologically justified will often concede that the opposite case has its strengths. When biblical evidence for infant baptism is lacking and its administration for centuries results in our present pagan society, arguments against the practice carry weight. Similarly, everybody today pays lip-service to the priesthood of all believers (even though they may ordain priests) and to religious liberty (even though they may once have opposed it). There is therefore a readiness to accept some elements of Baptist identity.

But this is rarely true of the Baptist approach to church

government. Neither the established and historic denominations nor the new churches of the restoration movement express appreciation of this part of the witness. Indeed, objections to it are frequent, and relate to the principle and the practice of government by church meeting.

As regards the principle, it is claimed, first, that it is *unbiblical*. Those who take this view argue that authority in the New Testament was invested in apostles and in the elders whom they appointed. The missionary practice of Paul and Barnabas is indicated in Acts 14:23: 'Paul and Barnabas appointed elders for them in each church and, with prayer and fasting, committed them to the Lord in whom they had put their trust.' Elders are said to 'direct the affairs of the church' (1 Tim 5:17) and the church is told they are 'to respect those who work hard among you, who are over you in the Lord and who admonish you' (1 Thess 5:12).

Hebrews 13:17 is even more explicit: 'Obey your leaders and submit to their authority. They keep watch over you as men who must give account. Obey them so that their work will be a joy, not a burden, for that would be of no advantage to you.' Authority in the church appears from these verses to be vested in eldership figures, whether in the external bishop or apostolic minister, or in the local leadership. How then can the democratic form of government represented by Baptist churches be squared with the Bible?

A second criticism is that the Baptist approach is *unspiritual*. This is on several counts. It is unspiritual because it treats all members of the church as if what they have to say is equally important. The new convert or the backslidden member have equal rights to a voice in the church meeting as the most spiritual and wise. Furthermore, the church meeting dispenses with the spiritual discipline of submission whereby, in placing ourselves under the authority of a duly appointed leader, we crucify our own pride and rebelliousness and learn meekness.

In place of this, the church meeting substitutes the lawless attitude and spiritual anarchy of everyone doing what is right in his own eyes (Judg 21:25). This is demonstrated by the worldly voting procedures followed in church meetings, which are not scriptural, create a sense of confrontation, are a form of power game, impose the will of the majority on the minority and often produce bizarre results. All of this is more suited to a party-political conference than to the household of God.

Thirdly, church meetings are *impractical*. They have an inbuilt conservative bias which prevents the church responding swiftly or imaginatively to any initiative. They require that the church adapt itself to the pace of the most unwilling, unspiritual or disenchanted member. The church is therefore doomed to be limited in its growth because it will not allow a leadership style which is better adapted for larger churches. Such a system cannot allow for adventurous, strategic leadership because it gives excessive power to the suspicious, the slow and the short-sighted.

Now, this is a powerful array of arguments, which we shall be hard-pressed to answer. Unfortunately it gets worse. It would not be so bad if Baptists could respond and say, 'But you haven't understood. Come and see, and we shall show you how well it works.' The fact is that there are too many examples of it working very badly, many others of it working in a mediocre fashion, and few of it working well. Some loyal Baptists will immediately dissent from this and tell us how well it functions in their neck of the woods. Usually this is said by people whose expectations are not high, whose particular church meeting functions to their personal satisfaction (and this could mean anything) or who are trying not to let the side down. Some few genuinely mean it and are an example to the rest of us.

To the criticisms of the church meeting in principle may be added the criticisms in practice which can call many witnesses for the prosecution. Among these would be the faithful retired minister who, to my knowledge, on his retirement vowed never to attend another church meeting in his life again. To his testimony would be added that of the many ministers for whom church meetings are to be dreaded because of their battlefield quality or for the opportunities for calculated opposition that they allow. For good measure, we might add the church meetings that have dismissed their ministers for no reason other than being too progressive.

Of course, the Baptist for whom church meetings can do no wrong will always find that the faulty boot is on the other foot. Most will acknowledge that there is some truth (at least) in what I am saying. Many others will add their agreement simply by not turning up because they do not like the atmosphere of church meetings.

In Baptist practice there is a yawning credibility gap which is going to take a lot of spanning. Those who are critical of Baptist ways know this and are right to draw attention to it. Pastors who belong to other networks of churches may admire many things in Baptist churches, but this is rarely one of them. It is considered one of the drawbacks of Baptist church life that the church meeting has to be contended with. It is not enough to adopt defensive attitudes that treat the church meeting as a sacred cow. It too must be criticised. Before we can hope to get anywhere better, we have to acknowledge the truth about the current state of play.

My experience is not untypical. The first church meeting I ever attended was something of a disillusionment. As it happens, I failed to realise that I should not have been there in the first place. Nobody told me until afterwards that I should have been a baptised church member first! The first thing to strike me was that the person who was doing most of the talking from the floor never actually attended church. He was a strong character and was being listened to with respect. He was a church member but not a member of the worshipping community. As I attended further church meetings I noticed that he was a faithful participant and invariably opposed the style and content of the pastor's preaching and leadership.

This experience taught me that there were problems both with the church meeting and with the concept of membership with which Baptist churches operate and which gave considerable power and influence to members who were not members in the true sense. Subsequent experience has confirmed that these were fairly typical problems, but it has done more than that. It has shown that church meetings can be either the low point or the high point of Baptist churches. I have been in church meetings which were as near to heaven in unity, agreement and fellowship as I expect to be this side of eternity. Church meetings are the high-risk zone of Baptist church life.

If a church can put its house in order at this point then it can do anything. It is precisely because *agreement* is what unlocks the dynamic of spiritual effectiveness that church meetings are such contested areas. The bottom line is that for them to work properly the people must be spiritually-minded. In the kingdom of God, no system can work properly without spirituality. The ideal for the churches is to have a system of government which is unable to work properly, or indeed to work at all, unless God is in it. Then we really would notice whether God is with us or not. The gathered church concept offers the possibility of such a system but it must be understood and we must be convinced about it.

The rest of this chapter is divided into four parts, in which I shall attempt with some care to construct an argument for a renewed understanding and practice of congregational government. It is unfortunate that to arrive at the desired destination we will need to make an occasional apparent detour. Because the journey may prove a little complex it may help to know where we are going.

First, we shall seek to remove certain misunderstandings about the gathered church concept. This is necessary for the sake not only of its critics but also of the advocates of the church meeting who sometimes have little understanding of what it stands for. Secondly, we need to identify what it is that has distorted Baptist practice and led it down a false path. We shall locate these distortions historically in the Victorian age and organisationally in a wrong understanding of church membership. Our concentration will rest for a time on whether the church is an organism, an institution or both.

Thirdly, our attention will turn to biblical arguments for

congregational church order. As this is so important and at the heart of Baptist thinking it will occupy some space. Fourthly, we shall deal with the practical reform of the present situation and shall attempt to develop guidelines for decision-making.

Clearing away the misconceptions

Saying something worthwhile usually involves the need to clarify. False impressions are easily gained. It is unfortunate when those who hold a point of view are themselves confused as to what it really means. This is undoubtedly the case among members of the average Baptist church and considerable education is required. Our intention here is to isolate misconceived ideas and correct them.

(1) We begin with the question of democracy, because it is often assumed that the rule of the people is what Baptist churches are all about. On the front cover of one book of Baptist history are the words: 'The story of a people who have sought to practise New Testament Christianity, defend religious liberty, and foster the democratic way of life.' The book was intended for the American market and such an advertiser's blurb would be thought of, not surprisingly, as a good selling-point.

I want in a moment to argue that democracy is not the point, but before doing so wish also to say that even if it were, there are worse things than democracy. Only those in democratic countries could use the word as if it were a term of reproach. Democracy as a political system is certainly in part one of the fruits of Baptist witness and it should not be denigrated, as I have sometimes heard done from restorationist platforms, as if it were something inferior. This said, is Baptist church government democratic? The answer depends, of course, on the definition of democracy.

If by democratic we mean that the church is not an autocracy, a patriarchy, an aristocracy or an oligarchy and that nobody has (or should have) the power to dictate but that the freedoms of the people are respected, it is certainly democratic. Baptist church government from the human point of view resembles democracy more than anything else (except, very occasionally, anarchy!). If, to take another definition, democracy means that in the church the will of the people is supreme, it is not and can never be a democracy, since the will of Christ who is the Head of the church may alone be given this position. If anything, the church is a theocracy, a people who are ruled by God.

But often when people describe it in this way the deduction they draw is that therefore the elders, or the bishop, or the Pope should rule since this is more theocratic. This does not follow. There is no reason why the rule of one or a few in the church should be considered any more theocratic than democracy. All these systems may be quite wrong or inadequate. The rule of elders is as likely to obscure the rule of God as is the rule of the people, since we are all flesh. The government of the church fits into none of these easy categories. A statement on the doctrine of the church issued by the Baptist Union in 1948 put it like this:

> The church meeting, though outwardly a democratic way of ordering the affairs of the church, has a deeper significance. It is the occasion when, as individuals and as a community, we submit ourselves to the guidance of the Holy Spirit and stand under the judgments of God that we may know what is the mind of Christ.[6]

Some of the phrases used here are helpful. It is not the intention of church meetings to find out what the majority want and give it to them. We are concerned with 'the guidance of the Holy Spirit', 'the judgments of God' and 'the mind of Christ'. The question becomes for church meetings 'What does God want?' rather than 'What do we want?'. There is a shift of perception in these words away from democracy to discernment. The key factor in the government of the church is understanding what the will of the Lord is. All of this means that the government of the church has a unique character which does not correspond exactly with any human system.

Karl Barth's description of the church as a 'brotherly Christocracy'[7] expresses this unique character, although it should be amended to a 'brotherly and sisterly Christocracy'. The church is a community of friends among whom Jesus Christ rules and with whom he shares his heart and mind by the Spirit. It has a unique character and church members ought to be made fully aware of this, otherwise they will tend to behave as if it were simply a democracy.

It must be questioned whether the human procedures of formal decision-making are appropriate to this unique form of church life. The paraphernalia of voting and constitutional method can create an atmosphere which is quite at variance with seeking the mind of the Lord, for which prayer and worship are more fitting. To this point we shall return. Our conclusion is that it is misleading to think of the church as a democracy. We agree with P.T. Forsyth that congregationalism 'was the mother of political democracy but not its child'.

(2) We turn to the misconception that church government by church meeting implies that everyone's opinion is equally valid. This may be a concomitant of the democratic practice of giving each person an equal vote irrespective of age, wisdom or ability. The view that no one opinion is better than another does appear to be the bottom line of a voting system. If the character of a church meeting is changed, however, so that it becomes an occasion for discernment rather than for democracy then it becomes clear that not each voice carries equal weight.

Those who have been called and recognised to shepherd the flock, those who are mature in faith, those who are prayerful and live close to God and who know and understand people, will all have particularly weighty contributions to make to the discernment process. They should be listened to with care and respect. Church meetings, properly understood and led, are occasions for sharing wisdom, not for airing prejudices or defending preferences. Yet because the Spirit is wont to speak in unexpected ways, wisdom cannot be confined to the mature. The prophetic word can come from the mouths of spiritual babes and infants and therefore some forum in the life of the church which enables this to happen is essential.

(3) This leads on to a third misconception, which has to do with the episcopal and presbyterian insights which we have already discussed. Congregational government does not exclude the presbyterian insight that within any church there are those who serve in leadership, nor the episcopal view that there are persons outside the local church whose spiritual oversight is desirable. What it does affirm is that no such persons are able to exercise an effective spiritual ministry unless that ministry is willingly received from below by those people who constitute the church.

There are several points here, one of which has to do with the nature of spiritual authority. Such authority comes from God and is the result of knowing him and being called by him to a specific function in the body of Christ. As the Son has been sent by the Father and has his authority, so the Son sends his servants and they share in the authority he has from the Father (Jn 13:20; 20:22–23). This is a very high view of Christian leadership. But God's kind of authority, seen in Jesus, is not one that compels by force but wins through love.

For this reason, true authority must not only be given from above but accorded recognition from below. Only when willing acceptance from God's people is present can there be an exercise of true spiritual authority. Congregational government does not deny the authority of those who are called as if it were nothing. It receives it gratefully, accords it place and enables it to come to expression. Because the church is a free community we cannot get away from this element. Even in churches where there are elders or bishops, it must always be the case that those who follow add their consent to being led. They cannot be compelled.

This was true even in the early church. The apostles could only minister in situations where they were freely received. They had no power to compel but only to persuade. It is because this is always the bottom line for the legitimate and

Christian use of authority that the congregation. churches has grasped a principle of the first order. church receives and respects those who are called them free to fulfil the tasks for which they have been c. God.

(4) This disposes of a further misconception along the way, namely that all decisions, however trivial, need to be approved by a church meeting. If the task of a church meeting is first of all to recognise and affirm those who are able to make responsible decisions on its behalf, it is by definition entrusting to them authority in the areas that are their agreed brief and which are consistent with the faith and the agreed policies of the church. It will also recognise that there are areas which are not clear cut and require particular discretion.

(5) It should not take long to dispose of the misconception that the church meeting always gets things right. Something is not right just because the meeting determines that it should be. What is true, however, is that church meetings (and all human enterprises) can only ever operate within the light that they have. As the light is inevitably limited so are the decisions we make. Moreover, there is such a thing as the right to get something sincerely wrong which is often a stepping-stone to greater wisdom.

(6) The final misconception we shall address is one which is more prevalent among Baptists than outside their ranks. It is the belief that there is only one structural way of expressing the congregational principle of government and that is through the institution of the church meeting. On the contrary, I would argue that it is possible to have an institutional church meeting and yet completely betray the principle of the gathered church. Conversely it is entirely possible to be true to the principle of the gathered church without ever holding a formal church meeting of the traditional type.

The development of this is that there are many denominational Baptist churches which may not be truly Baptist and many truly Baptist churches which are not denominationally Baptist. Paradoxical though this may sound, it is a necessary point and revolves around the question of when a Baptist church is a Baptist church. Apart from doctrinal issues, a church is generally considered by Baptist denominational bodies to be Baptist if it manifests certain institutional phenomena, supremely a formal church meeting. Thus when there is apprehension that Baptist distinctives may be eroded (as for instance through churches being influenced by the restoration movement) the tendency is to defend these institutional phenomena as if they were the essence of what we are about. The church meeting becomes the rallying-point. It must be defended at all costs.

Some of us reject this as being both hollow and shallow. It is hollow because it fails to recognise the extent to which the church meeting has been corrupted and is insufficiently self-critical. It is shallow because it makes the institution the essential issue *rather than the values on which the institution is supposed to be based*. The institution must itself be criticised when it falls short of the values to which it is supposed to bear witness. When church meetings become places for political power struggles and betray values of love and freedom, it is not enough to say that this is a true Baptist church because, even though corrupt, it still has a church meeting. In fact, it has betrayed itself and its heritage. This rather involved discussion now leads us to seek to discover how current practice has become distorted.

Discerning the distortions

We shall come straight to the point. Historically, major distortions entered into Baptist church life in the nineteenth century as churches grew away from their roots and, flourishing as they were in numbers, power and prosperity, made certain accommodations.

At one level, they accommodated themselves to the style of the established church. Increasing in self-confidence, they reflected in their architecture and ways of worship a major shift. Previously they had gathered in simple meeting houses.

Now they began to build huge cruciform Neo-G
conceived after the model of the parish church and co
with all that was culturally necessary for a nonconform
beginning to rival the establishment in earnest.

At another level, they paralleled the developments in
municipal and urban life, leading to the growth of societies,
institutions and organisations modelled on the democratic
pattern. The removal of religious restrictions increased nonconformist access to public life and its ways. Developments in
constitutional procedures in secular institutions were followed
by the churches. In the early days of the Baptist movement,
the concern of the church meeting as reflected in early minute-
books was the discipling of its members. Church meetings
were held immediately after church worship on Sundays. In
the nineteenth century the shift was away from discipling
towards business.

It seems to me that the heart of this distorting effect has to
do with the introduction of a false concept of membership
from which Baptist churches have still to recover. Many,
indeed, have still to recognise it. It is not that it was deliberately introduced, but that a subtly different approach to membership insinuated itself into the churches by force of
circumstance and lack of vigilance. Current concepts of membership need to be subjected to biblical and theological scru-
tiny and challenged with the question 'How scriptural is our
practice?'.

My argument is that our current systems of membership
are, by and large, shaped more by the demands of our secular
state for legal regularity than by the word of God. In order to
do things decently and in order within our society, the individual community of believers must of necessity assume a form
and double as a legal corporation within that society. To own
property, raise mortgages, receive and administer funds
responsibly, churches assume a legal status and identity. The
gravitational pull of this demand is that the church moves
from being a charismatic-organic community determined by

re to being an organisational-institu-
...ined by the legal criteria of society. In
are the seeds of some distortions which
...ted in the following areas.

...s created in our understanding of the
...t of church membership is well-rooted in
...s out of an organic model which sees the
chu... ...g body of Christ, guided by the Head and
activated by ... ...pirit (Rom 12:4–5; 1 Cor 12:12–13, 27). In
this sense, church membership is neither a choice nor an
option—it is an inherent part of Christian existence. It is not
something to be applied for or to be admitted to. It is a given.
In scriptural terms, being a member means being a redeemed,
functioning part of the new community. It is a functional
reality rather than a legal status.

Nowhere is the distinction between the biblical model and
much current practice so clearly perceived as in the kind of
church meeting where 'members' who are not functionally
part of the local body (and may not even attend worship)
appear to exercise their constitutional right. By the criteria of
Scripture such members are not members, or if they are, are
in a backslidden state which deprives them of an authentic
voice within the congregation. By the criteria of the secular
society and the legal corporation, they are members with all
the rights and privileges that this entails. The root of the
distinction to be made is that the church is not a club but a
covenant people.

(2) This distortion in understanding the church is accompanied by a similar one in the area of decision-making. The
purpose of membership is not seen as belonging to one
another in living service but as a convenience rendered necessary by the institution. To run this kind of democratic institution you have to have members. In the absence of bishops
who call the tune, some other controlling form of legal oper-
ation is required, that is, members. The church meeting is
thus transformed by the institutional gravitational pull from
being a discerning community seeking to find the mind of the

Lord into a meeting of shareholders out to protect their interest.

For this task two things are necessary. A suspicious and paranoid mentality views any new initiative as an attempt to defraud the shareholders of their traditional rights. A legalistic, barrack-room lawyer's knowledge of the constitution and procedural customs enables blocking tactics and delaying actions to be deployed. This is a long way from the kingdom of God. There are those who feel it almost a duty to take the role of opposition, sometimes on the ground that someone has to play devil's advocate—an odd idea if ever there was one!

One of the challenges facing Baptist churches is to discover biblical models of decision-making which transcend the normal, human patterns. The biblical picture is one where authority sometimes resides with the congregation (Acts 6:3); sometimes with the elders (Heb 13:17); sometimes with a perceptive individual (Paul against Peter—Gal 2:11ff); sometimes with a prophet (Acts 11:28); sometimes with the immediacy of God's word to a gathering (Acts 13:1–3); and sometimes with the considered mind of leaders and people in harmony with what appears to be the mind of the Spirit (Acts 15:28).

Perhaps the nearest definition we can give to this indefinable process is to see it as a godly consensus which searches and waits for the word of the Lord. It is a long way from the kind of gathering which, having gathered a small section of the worshipping membership, preoccupies itself with resolutions, amendments and counter-resolutions.

(3) A further distortion is in our understanding of church discipline. Discipline is far more than a periodic revision of the church roll, with suitable leniency towards those who are related to existing members of the congregation. Such an approach is orientated towards the question of who still has the right to vote. Biblical discipline is orientated to our spiritual walk and our conformity to Christ. It has to do with discipling, drawing people into greater faithfulness to Christ

as Lord. To become a member of a church is to submit oneself to the loving corrective admonition of its members.

Much of the distortion of Baptist church life can be seen from what has been said to have its origin in a defective view of membership. We are faced therefore with the task of the renewal of the concept of membership and of the actual membership of Baptist churches. There is plainly no substitute for a biblical renewal of understanding concerning the nature of the church and its membership, discernment and discipline. There is equally plainly no alternative but to adopt *some* legal and constitutional form if communities of believers are to administer finance, own property and observe the proprieties of society.

The best we can work for is to minimise the distortion that such institutional forms will tend to produce and to do so on the basis of a clear and convinced understanding of the true nature of church membership. What are the alternatives before us?

One possibility is to abolish the whole concept of constitutional membership and to establish communities which relate organically. The only way to become a member of such a community would be by being a member of the body. With this model, membership would not be a matter of satisfying a certain procedure of entry but of a joining of hearts and minds. It would rely on a declaration of commitment and would cease automatically if this commitment were withdrawn. The focus in this model would be upon the quality of relationships between individuals and the community rather than on the formality of being a member. Shorn of the constitutional element, decision-making would be conceived of more in consensus terms, with an individual's contribution being weighed by the quality of its content rather than on a one-member-one-vote basis.

Certainly, such a model would have justification in scriptural terms, since Baptist forms of membership lack support in the example of the early church. But it would have distortions

of its own once it adopted some institutio
need for the sake of legality to locate power
office-bearers or its trustees, which could proc
balance of power. Power would be concentrate
of individuals rather than more safely diffuseo
people and this would not be good for their souls
else's. A further feature which is observable in pract.   ~that
churches which do not have a formal membership may lack an
element of bonding in commitment between the people.
Those who easily come into the church may as easily depart
from it.

Despite this, and accepting that there are ways of remedy-
ing or reducing these defects, this model of membership offers
some creative possibilities, but only when operated by folk
who have the right values at heart. Despite what the cynics
might say, such people do exist.

A second alternative, which might provide more fruitful
possibilities, would be to refashion membership in a covenant,
as opposed to a constitutional, direction. This would be to
mark a return to the understanding of membership which
predominated in the first two centuries of English Baptist life.
The rationale of this approach is that every Christian belongs
to the body of Christ, but a local church is only formed when
individuals come together in an express commitment to walk
together and watch over each other in the Lord. For this
commitment to be expressed in some formal and clear way is
necessary both because it strengthens the bonds of fellowship
and because it acts as a way of giving permission for the exercise
of spiritual oversight and, when need be, of discipline.

This explicit agreement is a covenant. In a voluntary community which takes seriously the freedom of the individual,
some such process is essential. The rediscovery of covenant
membership would help avoid the distortions we have mentioned.

The following practical steps might help towards its implementation.

(1) A period of catechism should be held for those seeking

...bership in order to explain fully its true significance. The procedure of automatic transfer from one church to another should be dropped, since this implies a commonality of under-standing between Baptist churches which can no longer be assumed. Instead, all new members should receive instruction and courteous notification should be given between one church and another when membership changes.

(2) Members should commit themselves to a simple cov-enant such as was once common among Baptists. One such older document began with the question 'Do you solemnly give yourself up to the Lord and to the church to watch over and be watched over, to perform all the duties and enjoy all the privileges of the house of God?'. If Baptist churches were to get back into the habit of expressing in words the kind of commitment involved in covenant membership, they would be standing in the tradition of their spiritual forebears. The advantage of these covenants is that they give substance to commitment and provide a basis for reminding people of their responsibilities should they weaken in faith.

(3) Ways should be found of making organic and organisa-tional membership co-terminous, either by a periodic mem-bership renewal or by causing membership to lapse automatically on non-attendance or non-involvement without good cause. It should be clear that membership of the institu-tion is entirely dependent on true spiritual commitment and that without the latter, the former is invalid. This would obviate the problem of non-attending members still exercising constitutional power.

In these ways it is possible to counteract the distorting influences at work in the churches. The temptations to distor-tion will always be there, but that is life. We must do what we can and whatever we do will have its risks. The practice of covenant membership to which we have referred deserves to be reactivated, although many churches will not have lost it completely, and some perhaps not at all. It is a way of building strength but must not become a high wall which is used to keep people out of the church or a huge hurdle to be crossed. The church is an open church. This is where it must be stressed again that true membership is a living relationship within the family of God.

There is a partial analogy with marriage. A good marriage is not formed by passing through a legal ceremony, as we all know. It has to do with loving commitment. But the outward form and declaration made before witnesses that we call marriage can often strengthen a relationship and even sustain it in hard times. We marry a person because we love them. Sometimes also we must love them because we are married to them. So in the church the declaration of commitment in membership can be an expression of love for God's people. It can also be the reason why we go on loving and caring and are held in fellowship when we might be inclined to depart. But it is meaningless when it is not preceded by the spiritual membership of which it is a formal expression.

To this end, the local church must never be a closed community, but one into which people may be drawn readily through the friendships which are of its essence. Membership is a way of drawing people more deeply into Christ, not keeping them at arm's length.

We have been seeking in this section to deal with the distortions of the gathered church principle which are apt to make people turn away from it. These distortions exist and are to be struggled against. Fairness leads us to point out that all forms of church life have their distortions. Episcopacy can degenerate to an elitist, autocratic arrogance on the part of bishops who see themselves as 'lords' in the church. Presbyterianism can atrophy into authoritarianism on the part of a powerful group of elders. Connexionalism can lose itself in bureaucracy.

I do not pretend that these are fair representations of these ways of being the church, but they are, or have been, in evidence from time to time. The fact that something good can be distorted does not mean that in its good and healthy form it is to be rejected—quite the opposite. It must be recovered, provided that in essence it is worth recovering. This is a way of saying, provided there is a valid theological case for its existence in the first place. This is the task we turn to next.

Beyond distortion

In the light of the difficulties indicated, can a genuine case still be made from Scripture for the congregational order of church government, alias the gathered church, alias the church meeting? If I believed the answer to this were no, I should neither be writing this book nor should I bother to be a Baptist. Bearing in mind what has already been said about distortions, I am persuaded that the Baptist way of being the church has grasped something which has its origin in Jesus and the gospel, and which cries out to be implemented in its true form, in so far as we are able.

In this section I hope to marshall my arguments for a form of local church life which sees the authority of Christ being diffused by the Spirit throughout the body and not only located in those who lead. In order to be systematic I will here outline and number four strands of argument, of which some will be subdivided into other points.

(1) The argument from Jesus

The first line of argument, and as far as I am concerned the strongest, comes from the teaching of the One who is now the exalted Head of the church and who therefore should be allowed to determine what it is. In turn, this area is subdivided into three points.

(a) Jesus' understanding of the church. The focus here is on the key passage in Matthew 18:15–20 and particularly verses 18–20, where Jesus tells the disciples, first, that whatever they bind on earth will be bound in heaven, secondly, that when they agree on earth about anything it will be done for them by the heavenly Father and thirdly, that where two or three come together in his name he is there in the midst. All these ideas

are connected and the connection is most clearly perceived if we approach these points in the reverse order.

(i) When does a church exist? Jesus says it exists when a group of people comes together in his name and he is in the midst. A valid church is constituted in this way. It is not dependent upon the approval of a bishop or a town council for its validity, but upon the presence of Jesus Christ, its Lord and its foundation. Jesus, however, uses the key words 'in my name', which should not be missed. It is not just any gathering which makes for a church, but one which is in harmony and fellowship with Christ and which is intentional, that is, which is deliberately meeting together in Christ.

The Jews believed that a synagogue could only be formed, and corporate worship could only proceed, when there was a certain quorum of Jewish men. Jesus says nothing about men and indicates that the only quorum which is needed is his presence in those who are in fellowship with him. Here is the church and to this concept the early Baptists sought to give expression through their idea of covenant, that is, the intentional coming together of believers in the name of Christ.

(ii) Jesus indicates that when believers agree together on earth about anything they ask, it will be done for them by the Father (v19). It is important to remember that all such requests are only regarded if they are in the name of Christ, which means in harmony with him. We must also ponder here the meaning of 'agree'. There are different degrees of agreement and I suggest that Jesus is referring here not to people chancing on an agreement together, but to a deep, heartfelt unity of purpose and desire.

This is the unity of the Spirit in the bond of peace (Eph 4:3–5) and is a spiritual experience which opens up the door to the blessing of God. Where this spiritual agreement exists, the church has authority before God such that he will do whatever is so asked. The local church functions at its maximum when not only its leaders but the whole body is in spiritual agreement. This is what church meetings, properly understood, are about.

(iii) Such a church, meeting in the name of Christ, possesses an authority towards its members in addition to, and in dependence upon, its authority before God. This is indicated in verse 18, where the church is told that it is able to bind or to loose, which means to allow or to disallow in accordance with the Scriptures. It is competent therefore to make decisions which will be owned by God and to exercise authority on his behalf. Here is the foundation of the belief that authority in the church belongs to the whole of the gathered community and not exclusively to some within it. This brings us to a further area of Jesus' teaching.

(b) Jesus' understanding of church discipline. In fact much of Matthew 18 is about the unbounded forgiveness that the church is exhorted to demonstrate. The parables of the lost sheep and the unforgiving steward are both found in this chapter, one speaking of the love of the Father who goes seeking after the lost (vv10–14) and the other of his forgiving grace and the responsibility of the forgiven to forgive (vv21–35). These words should be noted before any reference to church discipline is made.

The church is a community of infinite forgiveness, yet occasionally it must take action about the member who has rejected exhaustive attempts to win them back from an unworthy life. Jesus speaks of this in verses 15–17 and says that when all else fails, the church has authority to exclude the sinful member from its fellowship. That such action was to be something other than a form of psychological violence is indicated by the words of Paul in 1 Corinthians 5:4 about just such an extreme case. It is when 'the power of the Lord Jesus is present' that the church has authority so to act.

The point to notice in the teaching of Jesus for the issue in hand, however, is that discipline is applied in ascending degrees of severity. The individual must be spoken to privately first of all. If this fails, one or two others are to become involved. If this fails, the most that could be done, than which there was no higher action, was that the whole church should be told and, if necessary, should act. This indicates that for

Jesus the gathered community, the congregation, was the highest court of appeal. The reason for this may be discerned in the following point.

(c) *Jesus' understanding of leadership*. Jesus rejected hierarchical, elitist and authoritarian approaches to Christian leadership and urged his disciples to do the same. This is at its clearest in Matthew 23:8–12 where he tells his followers that they are not to be called 'rabbi', 'father' or 'teacher', because they have one master and Father in God and one teacher in the Christ. Moreover, 'you are all brothers' (v8) and 'the greatest among you will be your servant' (v11). All forms of self-exaltation are inappropriate in the community of which he is the founder (v12).

For most of its history, much of the church has chosen to ignore these words completely and do the precise opposite. Jesus intended to form a community in which the supremacy of God within it was not to be eclipsed by the perennial human tendency to seek for status and position. It is the concept of the gathered church which has most potential for coming close to this, diffusing as it does the authority of Christ throughout its members. Such a community is both most able to check the self-exalting pretensions of its members and to give place to Christ in the midst. It is the simplicity of the gathered church that most seems to be in harmony with the teaching of Jesus.

(2) The argument from the New Testament theology of the church

What is taught by Jesus is confirmed by the theology of the church and of the Christian life contained in the New Testament. We refer to five areas to make this point.

(a) The New Testament teaches that *Jesus Christ alone is the Head of the church* (see Ephesians 4:15 and Colossians 4:18). Everybody accepts this in principle but not all agree on its implications. For Christ to be the Head means that the church in all its parts is organically related by the Spirit to Jesus Christ, who is the One from whom it draws its spiritual life. No other person or group of persons fulfils this function and the living headship of Christ should not be obscured by the belief that he uses intermediaries to transfuse his life to the body. His government is exercised directly over each part and not mediately through a system of delegates. This argues for a form of church life which allows for the direct government of the Head to be expressed.

(b) The New Testament teaches *the priesthood of all believers* (see 1 Peter 2:5, 9). This is the same truth as the last, expressed from below. All have direct access to the Head without the need for priestly mediation. This necessarily involves insight by the Spirit into God's being and purposes, in such a way as to impart to the believer the mind of Christ (1 Cor 2:9–16). This being the case church life should give opportunity for that which is known of the mind of Christ to be expressed.

(c) Similar to this is the teaching of *the anointing of all believers*, to be found in 1 John 2:20, 27. John teaches that those who believe have an anointing from the Holy One and therefore 'all of you know the truth' (v20). He then makes an astounding claim:

> As for you, the anointing you received from him remains in you, and you do not need anyone to teach you. But as his anointing teaches you about all things and as that anointing is real, not counterfeit—just as it has taught you, remain in him (v27).

John is here counteracting the influence of false teachers who were claiming to have true knowledge and calling into question the competence of the believers to know the will of God. His response is to affirm what they have already known of the preaching of the gospel and confirm that the anointing they have received from the Spirit remains in them. They may therefore trust their judgement in spiritual things over against those who make exclusive claims to have the truth.

(d) These last two points are strengthened by the New Testament stress on *the ministry of all believers*. Priesthood has two dimensions. It brings access to God and the ability to minister from God to his people. This forms the foundation of Paul's teaching on spiritual gifts in 1 Corinthians 12: 'Now to each one the manifestation of the Spirit is given for the common good' (v7). Among the gifts listed are those of wisdom and knowledge (v8) and prophecy and distinguishing between spirits (v10). As these gifts may be manifested through any believer as the Spirit chooses, it points towards the access of all to the discernment and decision-making processes of the local church and to the fact that all may serve in the body in these respects.

(e) The final area, which is concerned with the nature of the Christian life, is much neglected. It concerns *the ability to make godly decisions*, which is the goal and the mark of spiritual maturity. This particularly relates to Hebrews 6:11–14, where the author admonishes the Hebrew Christians for the immaturity that causes them still to need milk as though they were spiritual children. He then says, 'But solid food is for the mature, who by constant use have trained themselves to distinguish good from evil' (v14). The ability to make ethical judgements and decisions is the mark of the mature Christian.

This conflicts with the attitude of those who say that the mark of maturity is the willingness to submit to the decisions which others make on our behalf. The result of this approach is to produce immature Christians who know how to do what they are told but not how to think. Is this what we are about? How will we bring folk to maturity within the community of faith if we do not engage them, as an intrinsic part of their commitment, in the task of making good decisions? All should learn to take their part in the government of the local church.

(3) The argument from the example of the early church

New Testament theology does not stay in the realm of theory but is expressed in the actual kind of life we find the early church living. It is not part of our case in any of this chapter to argue that all the decisions of a church should only be made by the whole congregation. This is a recipe for total disaster and does not square with what we see in the early church. The spirit of confidence and trust and the work of the Spirit mean that there was a freedom in decision-making that enabled the church to advance swiftly. What we do find is that at certain times and for particular reasons the agreement of all God's people was necessary for strategic reasons and that the people were trusted to share in the decisions. We see this on three particular occasions:

(a) *Acts 6: 1–7* Here we find the church in Jerusalem experiencing difficulties which threatened to divide those who were Hebrew-speaking from those who spoke Greek. Jealousy and suspicion were erupting and the fact that the apostles were Hebrew speakers themselves did not help. Their solution was to gather 'all the disciples together' (v2) and to hand over to them the responsibility of choosing seven men who would help to maintain the unity of the church through impartial service. The type of person to be chosen was determined by the apostles but the actual choices were made by the church. It would have been interesting to know how they did it, but we are not told. We do know that the apostles left the decision to the people, blessed and worked with it when it was made and that the church increased all the more as a result (v7).

This is an example of congregational decision-making and was to do with the crucial matter of appointing leaders. The situation was tricky because of the potential divisions, but the decision was wise. Those chosen were all Greek-speaking (v5) and would command confidence from the part of the church which felt neglected. Incidentally, the Hebrew Christians who were involved in the decision showed grace and wisdom in giving space to the Greek speakers. The whole thing is an example of practical wisdom on the part of the apostles and the church, and a possible model for action today.

(b) *Acts 11:29–30.* Here we find the church in action, responding to a specific need. The prophet Agabus predicts that there is to be a famine and the disciples in Antioch make the decision, apparently spontaneously, to contribute money, each according to their ability, to help the church in Judea. Here is an example of a creative initiative emerging from the body of believers in response to a need. It appears that they also made the decision to send their gifts to Jerusalem by the hands of Saul and Barnabas (v30), for whom this was part of their development in ministry.

(c) Acts 15:1–35. Here we find a very difficult situation which was one of the major hurdles in the early church. It concerned the reversal of all the Jewish prejudices with which the church began and the inclusion in the church of Gentile believers on equal terms with Jewish. An ecumenical council was necessary to discuss it and was held in Jerusalem. We find the apostles and elders engaging in debate and coming towards certain conclusions designed to admit the Gentiles and make table fellowship between Jews and Gentiles possible.

It is not surprising that the apostles and elders of the church took the lead in the debate because of their calling, experience and understanding, but then we read in verse 22: 'Then the apostles and elders, with the whole church, decided to choose some of their own men and send them to Antioch with Paul and Barnabas.' The church in question is the church in Jerusalem which, after the expert deliberations, has been brought into the discussion and seems to be affirming its conclusion. Once more, there is care in appointing responsible people (Paul, Barnabas, Judas, Barsabbas and Silas) to represent them.

These examples show us a church which is creatively involved in responding to the Spirit of God, even to the extent of making decisions which affected its leadership, its programme, its very nature and its future. They are affirmative of a flexible model of congregational decision-making but not of one that requires that every decision, however small, must be approved by the body of the church. Within the context of the apostolic faith handed to them, we find the church being involved in making strategic decisions of policy at certain times and then of leaving the executive outworking of them to the responsible individuals whom they recognised.

(4) The argument from Christian freedom

Because the Christian gospel is about the freedom which is given us in Christ, freedom in all its aspects must be a value to which the church is tenaciously committed. Paul's exhortation in Galatians 5:1 not to submit again to a yoke of slavery because Christ has set us free should always ring in our ears. There are many yokes of slavery which present themselves as servants of freedom. The one which Paul had in mind was the yoke of legalistic religion which taught people that they could gain acceptance by God only if all the demands of the law were kept.

Paul's experience had taught him otherwise. The law had taught him his inability to fulfil its demands. It had been the means of awakening his sense of utter condemnation and guilt. But in Jesus Christ, he found God coming to him to accept him in grace, in spite of his inability to live according to the law. For the first time, he was liberated to be what God willed him to be. From then on he resolved that nothing other than Christ should control him, because only in Christ was there true freedom.

This freedom has many ramifications but they all amount to this: we are never to allow anything other than Christ to have dominion over our lives, whether this be a religious law, a political power, a domineering personality or an ecclesiastical organisation. In the last analysis, anything which controls us other than Christ will enslave us. Only in Christ do we find the end for which we were created and the fulfilment of all our existence. 'In him was life and that life was the light of men' (Jn 1:4). This is basic Christian truth and it has enabled generations of Christians to face persecution and oppression knowing within themselves an inner freedom which no power could take away from them. This is our heritage in Christ which Paul insists we do not betray.

What is the relevance of this for the form of the local

church? Quite simply, it means that church order must be so constructed as to enhance the freedom of the Christian. Because freedom is to be celebrated, and not begrudged as though it were a regrettable necessity of life, it must be a foundational principle for the fashioning of church order. People join a church voluntarily but do not then lose their freedom. They go on belonging to that church because they freely will to do so. A church's life, then, is built upon the ongoing consent and agreement of its members. This is why the model of mutual submission can form the only appropriate model for the church. People freely agree in Christ to lay aside their prejudices and their preferences for the sake of serving and preferring one another in love.

Submission is good if it means that I curb my selfishness and learn humility. But it cannot be good if it means that I am required to give up my freedom, and my responsibility as a free Christian to discern, in favour of unquestioningly accepting somebody else's point of view. This becomes an acute form of bondage. Submission can only work where two agree to walk together. This is what the congregational order of the church seeks to safeguard and express. In this respect it is both noble, because of what it seeks to guard, and realistic because in matters of true religion people cannot be compelled.

The church is a fraternal, not a paternal, community. These words are especially directed towards the restorationist churches with which Baptist Christians such as myself have so much in common. It is notable that the inherent soundness of many restorationist leaders, and the realism of the spiritual life, has led them back to a sometimes unconscious re-appreciation of congregationalism, without losing the stress on the need for strong leadership which belongs to their ethos.

This puts them within a whisker of many Baptist churches coming from a traditional background into a renewed life. Time has brought to light sufficient examples of the damage that is done when the attempt is made to deprive people, even with good intentions, of their spiritual freedom. There are enough people for whom entry into a Baptist church from a restorationist background has been like a great step into freedom to prove this point. We are all wiser. Hopefully, we are all more committed to the need to be free, and to be allowed to make freely on our own the decisions which concern us, or freely in fellowship those which concern our church community.

Taken together these assembled arguments furnish a powerful case for the concept of the gathered church. They need to do so in order to encourage us to overcome the distortions of the past. When something gets misshapen it may be that the best course of action is simply to get rid of it, and that without too much fuss. But when it is inherently valuable it is a tragedy not to restore it. Because there is a strong biblical and theological case for the gathered church, it is worth the effort (and it is an effort) of trying to put it right. It will require hard work, but first it will require hard thinking, and that is the subject of the next and final section of this chapter.

Redeeming the situation

We have previously argued that Baptist church life needs to undergo a series of shifts and that in the area of church government the required shift is from a constitutional to a consensus approach. Because government in the church is supremely to do with finding the mind of Christ and obeying it, voting as a means of decision-making is a blunt and inadequate instrument. This is true for a number of reasons.

First, it is reminiscent of a form of adversarial politics where one side is proposing a motion and the other opposing it, with the majority winning the day. It is questionable even in secular politics whether this is healthy—it is certainly not in the church. Secondly, it places the focus upon the choices or preferences of the individual voters rather than upon the will of God. As a form of decision-making it immediately sets off on the wrong foot.

Thirdly, it requires very little or no spiritual effort to make it work. Fourthly, it favours the obstructive or disaffected member who is bent on putting obstacles in the way of legitimate progress. Such a person may be totally in the wrong in spiritual terms but be able to wreak havoc in constitutional terms because the presumption of constitutional procedures is always towards inertia and inaction. They have developed as a sophisticated way of checking power and preventing abuse. There are those who argue that precisely on this score they are necessary in the church because it is as prone to abuse of power as any other organisation. The temptation to power is undoubtedly there, but despite this there are two things wrong with this approach.

In the first place, the cynical assumption that the church meeting is about preventing the abuse of power immediately introduces a factor into the decision-making process which itself hinders the making of godly decisions. Discerning the mind of Christ happens when the Spirit is not grieved but when there is an attitude of love and trust. Those who take the watch-dog approach, or see themselves as the opposition party, immediately violate this process.

In the second place, there are more effective ways of challenging the abuse of power than to adopt an adversarial mode. Non-hostile, humble expression of concern and disagreement is more likely to be heard by a meeting than is tense opposition. Disagreement may be the voice of the Spirit, but if so it must be shared in a way that makes it possible for the discerning community to accept it.

As an alternative to making decisions through voting, I am advocating a new way which I call 'consensus', that is, sensing together what the will of God is and how it might best be served. As it happens, this is the form of decision-making employed by the Quakers, from whom there is much to learn at this point. It may also be called 'mutual consent', decision-making neither by voting and majority rule nor by unanimity (which is difficult to achieve and gives great power to individuals) but by the minority consenting to the majority proceeding, even if they are in disagreement about a particular issue.

Consensus decision-making is realistic. It recognises that it is not easy to make decisions. Ethical decision-making does not come easily to any of us and for this reason many want to opt out of it and hand over the responsibility to someone else. In recent trends towards more authoritarian church structures this is one of the factors at work. Many people just want to be told what to do without the pain of working it out for themselves. Yet decision-making is a responsibility so important that it cannot be left to a few.

Moreover, support for a given course of action will always finally depend upon people's willingness to support it. Where there is a common agenda there is more effective action. Where participation is assumed or emotionally coerced it will create lethargy or resentment. How then can a Baptist church find the more excellent way of consensus? I have a number of suggestions to make.

(1) A new way must be taught since there is no formation without education. Churches need to be taught that they are different, that they are discerning communities with responsibilities to decide. The kind of material already presented in this chapter should be taught and expanded. We should be made aware of the tendencies to seek power which are in all of us and that two primary attitudes are necessary for God's people. First, until we are totally committed to seeking only God's will we shall simply regurgitate our petty concerns. The voice of the Spirit is paramount. Secondly, until we have cultivated an attitude of mutual submission and trust, true dialogue will be impossible. People will only speak freely if they feel they will not be threatened or embarrassed for holding a contrary viewpoint.

This process of education is a major task as a moment's thought will disclose. In setting this agenda we are immediately exposing the lack of spirituality of many Baptist churches, but this is ultimately the size of the problem. Lack of spirituality is exposed precisely here. Those who shepherd the flock have a big job on their hands. But once adequate teaching has been given, it becomes possible to point out to people how and where they are falling short. For this reason, it is a helpful thing for a church to agree the standards it will employ in decision-making.

(2) Churches should make the decision that, in so far as it is possible, they should not use voting procedures but rely rather on consensus. This will have two results. First, it will remove from church meetings a subconscious pressure which dictates that at the end of the day sides must be taken over issues. The effect of this is that people prepare their positions and manoeuvre for advantage in preparation for the great divide. I have frequently observed that people behave in church meetings according to the buttons which are pressed. By the time the agenda has been published, the meeting started and the minutes read, sufficient buttons have been pressed to activate all the responses gathered from a host of committee or political meetings. In consequence, people who might otherwise act quite differently are almost inescapably caused to react in inappropriate ways. To lay aside voting procedures quite consciously changes this.

The second result will be to push people significantly towards a different mode of decision-making which requires them to focus on God and his will.

Now, I say voting should be avoided 'in so far as it is possible'. It may not be possible to avoid it altogether. An instance of this may be decisions which must be made and formally recorded for legal purposes. This is a concession to the procedures of our society. It may also be, however, that voting may occasionally be employed as a way of serving the consensus process without pre-empting it. Certain decisions, for instance, may be arrived at by consensus and for the sake of clarity (because of the importance of the decision) under-girded with a formal vote which would put them beyond doubt.

It may be that for certain kinds of decisions, voting is the best way of enabling people to participate meaningfully (for instance in the appointment of some leaders), but not necessarily all. It would be as unhelpful to forbid voting in any circumstance as it would be to insist on it in all. But the fact that in Christian freedom it may sometimes be useful does not mean that it should be considered normal. It should only be used exceptionally.

It is also a regrettable fact that there are times when consensus and trust break down and voting is the only alternative left to a church to resolve a difficult situation. When this happens it should be felt and said to represent a failure in love and fellowship. Yet it may function at best as a safety-net, preventing total breakdown, and at worst to disclose a division requiring a radical remedy.

(3) A new pattern of church meetings is required, the object of which is to blur the distinction between formal church meetings and other meetings of the church. If consensus is adopted as the mode of decision-making, then it needs to be asserted that such a process cannot be confined to monthly or quarterly church meetings, but embraces the entire life of the church. This is healthy because it makes decision-making continuous with the life of the church in worship and fellowship. Church meetings are like the tip of the iceberg. The process of thinking and discerning takes place all the time and comes to the surface on occasion in order to be formalised.

Another analogy might be that the church meeting is like a person's conscious mind reflecting upon the continual stream of thoughts and impressions emerging from the subconscious mind. All of the life of the church—preaching, teaching, learning, discussing, worshipping and the rest—is directed towards knowing and doing the will of God. Church meetings function as the time when these things come to the surface and are clarified.

It is instructive to remember that the early Baptists held their church meetings immediately after the regular Sunday morning worship. There was wisdom in this, since it preserved the continuity between worship and decision which is sometimes lost by placing a church meeting in the middle of the week. We need to recover this continuity, but in a way appropriate for our more mobile times. A number of things could help here. Church meetings need to be made more like other meetings of the church, and vice versa. In the next point we shall suggest how church meetings might be reformed in terms of content. Here we suggest how a new pattern of meetings might help.

For instance, imagine that an average Baptist church has a church meeting once a month. This could be altered to make only one of these meetings every quarter a formal church meeting and the other two, opportunities for prayer, with the emphasis on sharing thoughts, needs, frustrations and concerns. Decisions would not be made at this latter sort of meeting, which would rather allow for prayerful involvement of the people in the process of thinking that will lead to decision. People need to be involved in the making of decisions, not just in their approval.

These occasions could be times when questions are asked, opinions expressed and fears considered, without the pressure to decide there and then but with the emphasis on understanding before deciding. To understand fully makes decision-making much easier. Where people feel pressured to decide, they will resist.

Interestingly, new churches which have thrown out the church meeting have often reintroduced it by another name, such as Family Night or Fireside Chat. Under another name, these occasions seek to fulfil a similar function to church meetings, that is, sharing mutual concerns, imparting information, receiving feedback and taking the temperature. Yet because the atmosphere is informal and there is not the pressure to come to a decision or to take sides, open communication is made easier. Quarterly church meetings might then be occasions when this process comes to a head, decisions are clearly made and recorded and the church makes progress together.

To operate such a system it would be essential that the

eeting only deal with matters that it really needs to, matters of policy, personnel (particularly leadership nents) and general accountability. It would need to respect the executive actions of those whom it appointed to office and give them leave to operate. It would also need to give great respect to the advice and direction of those appointed to lead. But they in turn would have much greater opportunity to listen to those who are being led and this is one of the primary skills of leadership.

(4) The content and structure of church meetings must be reformed. Church meetings need to become more like other meetings of the church in that they should be primarily concerned with prayer, worship and learning. This is required by the search for consensus. If the supreme concern is to know the mind and will of God, worship and prayer in which we listen to him and wait upon him become crucial. It has been suggested that church meetings should be composed of five ingredients: worship, fellowship, vision-sharing, building faith and business. These are designed to lift the nature of church meetings into the realm in which they should operate, faith in the living God. Between these various activities many aspects of a standard church meeting might be distributed and communicated in a positive way. When this happens, the business of the church, that which must be decided, is seen in its proper context. All of this might take place within a framework of prayer and intercession. This is not a recipe for perfection but at least it is one which makes for progress.

(5) We need to acquire and develop skills which make for effective communication. Communication will often be mentioned as a problem faced by a church, particularly in a time of marked progress. In this we are of a piece with the rest of our society which struggles with the same lack of skills. I am thinking here of the ways in which information may best be communicated, but even more about the communication of feelings. How do we express things about which we feel deeply without becoming aggressive or defensive in our attitude? How do we say things which we instinctively feel will be

unpopular or against the stream? How can we be critical without becoming destructive or being disloyal?

We all need to learn skills which are healthily assertive and which do not come easily, perhaps even less so in our culture than in others. Think of the difficulty British people have in complaining in a restaurant! We either blow up and alienate those who are serving us or say nothing and fume, when a few words politely and frankly expressed would be for everybody's benefit. The church of Jesus Christ should be the ideal place to learn how to be graciously and generously direct. It might help us, for instance, if we learned how to speak from the heart and to say, 'This is how I feel about this.'

This enables us to be honest, but at the cost of making ourselves vulnerable, not of criticising others. Most people respect this approach and know instinctively how to distinguish between the genuine and the manipulative. Speaking from the heart avoids making or implying accusations about other people's motives and cuts through verbal point-scoring.

It is paramount that we rid ourselves of the competitive need to win or to have our own way. This is the true meaning of submission, the attitude which is prepared to let go of preferences and prejudices for the sake of love for sisters and brothers. It is this that people find so difficult, because they confuse issues of principle with issues of preference or of personality. The number of problems caused in the church by issues of ethical or doctrinal principle is insignificant compared with those which have to do with wanting things our way. To help people discern this is the task of leaders who have themselves learned the difference.

The problem with the Baptist way of being the church is that it cannot work as it should unless the people are learning to be spiritual. It may either be regarded as an idealistic dream or as a great challenge. Current practice among Baptists says something about the spiritual condition of the churches. It is here that the great Baptist credibility gap is to be found. What is at stake is not only the standing of individual churches but the insights concerning the nature of Christ's new community for which Baptist Christians stand.

These are not merely secondary matters which can be treated indifferently; they touch the heart of a gospel which speaks of a God who has come humbly as a servant to call us friends and to wash our feet. He has also called us to be like him, to discover a spiritual power for good by renouncing worldly ways of lording it over people. All of this belongs to the Baptist witness and it is up to us to do more than justify it defensively. We are called to prove it is Christ's way by living it out in the grace which he provides.

5

Renewing Association

Throughout this book we have been working with the assumption that there are two fundamental dimensions of the church, the local and the universal. It is essential to recognise that every local church is a part and expression of the universal church of Jesus Christ, and although the two might be distinguished for clarity's sake, they are never to be separated. Every Christian is under obligation to think universally when they think about the church. Universal and local interact and interpenetrate.

Much of what has so far been written has been about the life of the local church. I indicate in this my conviction that to be real it must be local. The Christian faith is not lived out in theory in some unreal universal ideal, but in reality among a group of local sinners who are being redeemed—among the good, the bad and the ugly. This is exciting because it is real, and irritating because it is difficult. It is therefore necessary that we think local, but the danger of this is that we become parochial, apt to imagine that the church begins and ends with our little congregation.

This is not healthy and ends up suffocating both us and the local church. We hold together the reality of the local and the breadth of the universal when we remember that each church community is a member of the wider church. Now this takes some thinking about because, not to put too fine a point on it, this church is in a mess. It is divided and it is confused.

One way in which Baptists have always thought it confused is in the way it thinks about itself. In the New Testament the church is quite simple. It is two-dimensional. It is the sum total throughout all space, time and history of those who belong to Jesus Christ, between whom there exists in heaven and on earth a bond called in the creeds the communion of saints. There are those who are alive in heaven (who have been called the church triumphant) and those who are alive on earth (the church militant) but it is universal and it is one (see for example, Ephesians 1:22–23 and Matthew 16:18). The other dimension is that the church is expressed in local geographical communities of those who believe (see Galatians 1:2 and Revelation 1:4).

To this simple and clear teaching, Christians have added two major misunderstandings. They have begun to use the word 'church' to refer to buildings in which the church gathers. This has obscured the truth so clearly stated in the New Testament that the church is people. Even Baptists have been carried away over this one, departing from their early and correct instinct to talk about meeting houses or chapels. Of course they make a mental note that they do not mean what they say when they refer to a building as a church, but the damage is done, the wrong impression is conveyed. It will only be undone when they find some other vocabulary to say what they really mean, such as 'worship centre'.

The second misunderstanding is to be noticed when denominations, or groups of churches, are called 'Church', as in 'Roman Catholic Church', 'Methodist Church', 'United Reformed Church' and the like. Here is a new understanding of the church which does not correspond with the New Testament for it gives the name of church to some organisation which is smaller than the universal and greater than the local. Occasionally even Baptists fall into this trap when they refer to the Baptist Church, meaning the Baptist denomination.

For years, the administration building of the Baptist Union was called Baptist Church House, which can only be described as a total misnomer since 'the Baptist Church' does not exist, except when we mean the Baptist church in a particular locality, or possibly a gathering of Baptist believers in some translocal assembly. The word 'church' is popularly but unhelpfully used to refer to a more or less centrally organised denomination, a use which is questionable both biblically and theologically.

It may be that this inadequate usage could be justified by saying that the less than ideal, divided state of the wider church means that less than ideal language must be used. What is of genuine and indisputable value, however, is that local churches have an enhanced appreciation of the wider dimension of church life when they belong to a network or fellowship of churches. If the local church is not to become isolated it must participate in some effective form of fellowship. The localism of the local church needs to be balanced by the catholicity of a wider grouping and of the whole, so that the local may be enriched by the whole. Whatever may be said of the name of such a grouping or the manner of its existence, it cannot be denied that such solidarity is biblical, helpful and necessary. Nor can it be denied that Baptists, with their bias towards the local, need to capture a new vision of the catholic and ecumenical.

Baptist Christians have used the word 'association' to describe their understanding of the way local churches should relate to each other. The intention of this chapter is to re-examine the concept and the practice of association. I am going to argue that the concept is excellent and needs to be re-appropriated, that the current practice of association leaves much to be desired, for reasons that I shall seek to specify, and that new patterns of association need to be worked out. In doing so I do not wish to lose sight of the fact that the process of renewal is already under way in this area and that many positive new developments are taking place.

The concept of association is one of the insights of the early

Baptists which captures something of the gospel. In the body of Christ we need each other. This understanding balances the emphasis we have already placed upon the competence of the local church. The picture of the church we were painting is one which views highly the autonomy of the local church, that is, the freedom of the local church to determine its own destiny without compulsion from outside.

This doctrine follows on from that of the freedom of the individual conscience and is the corporate expression of the same idea. As with the individual, so with the group. As it is wrong to force an individual to act against conscience, so it is wrong to compel a group to act contrary to that which it has determined to be right. The group may be wrong, but it has the right even to be wrong. Yet this principle may be taken to an extreme, to the assertion of independency or isolationism and the belief that a church exists without reference to, or care for, the body of Christ generally.

A truer attitude would be the recognition that we are all, individuals and churches, interdependent. The early Baptists used the word 'association' to describe this because, while it spoke of interdependence, it also implied that this could only be freely entered into and not compelled. Here we see the same principle operating on the corporate level as on the individual. As no religious acts had meaning unless they were freely entered into by the individual (voluntaryism), so corporate religious acts needed to be free to be real. Churches may freely associate together for mutual benefit but no church should have power over another. The only true power is that of love and mutual service.

This is the concept of association and it has been present among Baptists from the beginning. It amounts to an affirmation that whereas churches are competent to discern the mind of Christ and to administer their affairs, they are not omnicompetent and stand in need of other churches to aid them in their pilgrimage.

One of the earliest Baptist doctrinal statements was the Particular Baptist Confession of Faith drawn up by seven local churches in London in 1644. It affirms both the autonomy of the churches and their interdependence. For instance, article thirty-six (suitably modernised) asserts:

Being thus joined, every church has power given them by Christ for their well-being, to choose among themselves meet persons for elders and deacons, being qualified according to the word as those which Christ has appointed in his testament, for feeding, governing, serving and building up of his church and that none have any power to impose upon them either these or any other.

But article forty-seven reads:

And although the particular congregations be distinct and several bodies, every one a compact and knit city in itself; yet are they all to walk by one and the same rule and, by all means convenient, to have the counsel and help of one another in all needful affairs of the church, as members of one body in the common faith under Christ their only head.

A later confession (1689) repeats this point:

All members of each local church are engaged to pray continually for the good and the prosperity of all churches of Christ, wherever located, and upon all occasions to assist all other believers, within the limits of their own areas and callings, in the exercise of their gifts and graces. It follows therefore that churches should seek fellowship with one another, so far as the providence of God provides opportunity for the enjoyment of such benefits.

What this might mean is indicated in a further statement:

When difficulties or differences occur in respect of doctrine or church government and peace, unity and education are at risk, one church only may be involved, or the churches in general may be concerned. Again, a member or members of a church may be injured by disciplinary proceedings not agreeable to the truth and church order. In such cases as these, it is according to the mind of Christ that many churches in fellowship together should meet and confer together through their chosen representatives, who are able to give their advice on the matters in dispute to all the churches concerned. It must be understood, however, that the representatives assembled are not entrusted with any church power properly so called, nor have they any jurisdiction over the churches themselves to exercise discipline upon any churches or persons, or to impose their conclusions on the churches or their officers.

A picture is beginning to emerge. Churches are to fellowship with each other for the purpose of mutual support and correction, but this must not be allowed to become the exercise of power by one church over another or by a group of churches over a single one.

A helpful summary of early Baptist understandings of association is given in documents drawn up for the inaugural meeting of the Abingdon Association in 1652. After affirming that churches ought to hold 'a firm communion with each other', the statement is backed up by the argument that there is the same relationship between one church and another as there is between the members of one church. Just as each believer should be part of a church for the purposes of mutual support and correction, so churches should manifest the same care over each other. The aim is to keep one another pure by disowning those who are disorderly.

This love between churches is part of our love for all the saints and enables the work of God in which each church is engaged to be carried on. It enables churches to exhort, counsel and assist each other and convinces the world because it is the mark of mutual love by which churches are recognised as true churches. This understanding of the need to associate appears to have derived from a natural instinct on the part of early Baptists to seek for like-minded congregations. No doubt it was also expedient because they originated as a relatively small group and needed each other.

The early development of associations was hastened by political factors. Many early Baptists emerged between 1640 and 1660 at the time of the English Civil War during which the parliamentary forces, which they supported, were organised in regional associations. The influence of this upon early Baptists can be seen in the interchurch practices they adopted.

From a biblical point of view, the concept of association may be seen as a way of being true to the connections between the churches which we see in the pages of the New Testament. The early churches appear to have been loosely and organically organised by means of a network of relationships which may well be described as an autonomy within an interdependency.

We see this emerging between the church in Samaria and that at Jerusalem in Acts 8. When people responded to Philip's preaching, there was a delay in the manifest outpouring of the Holy Spirit upon them until Peter and John came down from Jerusalem to lay hands on the new believers (vv14–17). The clearest explanation of this delay is that it was important for the sake of unity in Christ for the Samaritan church to be organically related to the church in Jerusalem through the apostles. This was especially necessary in view of the long-standing hostility between Jews and Samaritans, and for them thus to receive the Spirit at the hands of Peter and John sealed the relationship with the church in Jerusalem.

In a similar fashion, when Gentiles in Antioch came to faith, the church at Jerusalem sent Barnabas to investigate the situation. He recognised it as a work of God and gave himself, with Saul, to teaching and training the people (Acts 11:22–26). Soon after, we find the church at Antioch sending financial aid to Jerusalem. There are other examples. In Acts 15, we read that representatives of the churches converged on Jerusalem to come to important conclusions about the relations between Jews and Gentiles in the church. Romans 15:26 tells us of contributions being made by the churches of Macedonia and Achaia for the poor in Jerusalem. In Romans 16:1–2, Paul commends Phoebe, who is a minister of the church at Cenchrea, to the Roman church.

A picture is forming of scattered churches reaching out to

each other in support and mutual affirmation, with the travelling apostles making connections between them and with at least one representative gathering taking place. The word 'association' appears to describe this process well. That it was not the establishing of a hierarchical organisation with the church in Jerusalem, or in Rome, acting as headquarters seems clear. The kind of relationship to exist between the churches and the apostles is well summed up by Paul in 2 Corinthians 1:24: 'Not that we lord it over your faith, but we work with you for your joy, because it is by faith you stand firm.'

Association is about working together with people and their churches (not dominating them) that their joy and faith might increase. It is about churches being in strong relationships so that they might support, correct and care for each other. It is about expressing the unity which we have in Christ. There is not much wrong with this concept. It is biblically, theologically and practically necessary.

So much for the issue in principle, but what about the practice? One thing to be recognised straight away is that because of the fragmented state of the church today, we are living in a different situation from the early church. The church of Christ is now divided into many parts and the extent of the disagreements between them makes it a hard task to put it all together again. We have to recognise that any expression of association today is going to be partial, and that the unity of the whole church is something that awaits us in the future, as God wills. However, the unity of the church must begin by seeking for association with those who are doctrinally closest to us, without our standing in condemnation upon those of other traditions.

From the beginning, Baptists have associated. But all is not well with the practice of association, even if the theory is right. We must determine at this point what has gone wrong and then we might consider if it can be put right. Inevitably we will be speaking here primarily of the denominational forms of life that have been developed by Baptist Christians. There are, for instance, some thirty-nine associations in England and Wales which are listed in the *Baptist Union Handbook*. We shall see, however, that although we shall begin with them, our attention will wander beyond them.

The present practice of association falls short of the meaning of the term. Some associations have been passing through difficult times. Some of the reasons are obvious. We see at work in association life, for instance, the same distorting institutionalisation which we have noted in the local church. Associations began with the desire for friendship and relationship. Churches entered into association with each other because of real and meaningful connections between them, having shared much and very often having derived from each other in the first place. In the course of time, the associations developed legal and institutional forms as ways of expressing the relations between the churches.

Eventually, however, the order came to be reversed, with the institutions growing in importance and the warmth of the relationships between churches waning. Here is a subtle shift and it is reflected in the rationale that is now often given for participation in associations. Churches are urged to relate because they are in an association, rather than to associate because they are in relationship. Of course, this is not wrong but it does mark a move away from the organic to the organisational, which needs to be recognised.

With this have gone other changes which have made it difficult for churches to sustain good relationships with each other. Over the centuries, Baptist churches have been influenced by the winds of doctrinal change so that a close original theological similarity can no longer be assumed. For the past hundred years it has no longer been the case that every Baptist church is firmly and convincedly evangelical. This makes association difficult and risks making associations into organisations of convenience rather than of theological agreement. Now, it is one thing to fellowship with believers of markedly different doctrinal positions and another to work closely together. The closer the working together, the more agreement tends to be necessary. The less the agreement, the less the degree of close association is likely to be.

It is, of course, possible to turn this into a virtue and argue that the value of associations is precisely that they bring people of different persuasions together. This, however, though true, sounds like an argument from necessity and runs counter to the original rationale for association, which was to bring together folk of like mind. It is an example of how institutions consider their own survival of prime importance, even if this means renegotiating the reason for their existence. That people of differing persuasions should be in dialogue together is admirable and desirable, but it does not constitute the relationship of mutual support and correction originally conceived as the basis for association.

To the growth of theological pluralism should be added other forms of diversity. Churches respond differently over the years to trends and currents in the spiritual life. At the moment this is most marked in relation to charismatic renewal, to which Baptist churches may be sympathetic, hostile or divided in attitude. Churches which share an evangelical faith may be pursuing quite different pathways at this point, with all the consequent difficulties for confidence, common worship and endeavour.

There are other trends which we may mention. Baptist churches differ in their appreciation of liturgical forms of worship, ecumenical enthusiasm and social action, and increasingly the dividing lines are falling in strange places so that stereotypes are difficult to isolate. The total effect of all of this is that belonging to an association by no means guarantees the reality of association. Association life in some places has declined and depends for its continued existence upon its legal and financial functions rather than on the fulfilment of a spiritual mission. This is by no means universally the case but in so far as it is, it constitutes a problem.

It is paradoxical that some good examples of what association can mean are found outside the Baptist denominations among the restorationist groups committed to a basically baptistic understanding of the church. I call this paradoxical because they are often regarded as a threat to what Baptists stand for. Some of these groups have worked hard to create and sustain supportive networks and it is not necessary to agree with every aspect of them to acknowledge what has been accomplished. It is for this reason that some Baptists have changed their allegiance to such groups. In doing so, they have not departed from previously held convictions but consider that they have found a more adequate expression of what they have always believed in.

This is most acutely felt by pastors eager to belong to a supportive and challenging coalition of like-minded leaders and churches. To leave an institution which is perceived (rightly or wrongly) to be unable to deliver what it believes in, in favour of a network which can and does, has seemed to them a responsible step. Some have attempted to combine membership of both the old institution and the new network, believing that each has something to offer which the other finds it hard to supply. One gives a sense of history, breadth and theological reflection, the other a sense of vitality and drive. It may be instructive to examine what is being offered by such networks.

First, they are non-institutional in the sense that local, autonomous congregations are not required to become affiliated to a legal body which then may act as a trustee of its premises or function in some other formal role. Secondly, they are relational, in that the emphasis is on the building of trust and confidence between leaders and churches and this leads to a sense of common purpose and accountability. Because these relationships are not given institutional form they remain voluntary and may be withdrawn from should this prove necessary.

Thirdly, they stress the need for relating churches to gather and in this way the sense of corporate identity is developed and expressed. These gatherings may include regional celebrations, national Bible weeks, and conferences for leaders or for training purposes. Fourthly, they are marked by a common philosophy of mission and ministry, which serves to impart a sense of purposeful identity and which is the source of practical insight into the building of strong churches. Like the early Baptists, they believe that church order is important and there is a consequent attention to the best ways in which churches may be built together.

This strengthens the sense of mutual aid and is practical. It means that participating churches may draw wisdom and help from a wider pool of churches, many of which have progressed further in the development of their own life. This contrasts with the state of affairs in more traditional Baptist circles, where innovation is more difficult to accomplish and sometimes carried through without outside support.

What I have described from observation of restorationist networks of churches could be accurately described as association. It is not the purpose of this book to evaluate restorationism but I do wish to argue that in certain respects this contemporary movement may act as a prophetic sign to Baptist Christians (and others) in the same way that Baptists may be a sign to the church as a whole. We need to heed its witness where necessary. In restorationist networks there is much that is good that can act as a stimulus for the recovery of a neglected heritage among Baptists. The renewal of association is one such area. The problem is not exclusively the excessive dose of independency in the churches, but the weakness of associations, as yet, in inspiring and facilitating organic relationships between the churches. So our attention turns to how a new experience, and possibly new patterns, of association may be discovered.

We are talking primarily about relationships. We do not need any new denominations because we already have more than we need. What we do need is for shoots of new life and growth to emerge in the shadow of the existing structures, receiving protection from them while they do so. The larger hope is that the whole of Baptist denominational life might undergo a transformation in which its institutions might be renewed. But this is a strategy which must be pursued through shorter-term objectives. What is now required is for association to become a reality by the forging of health-giving friendships between churches and their leaders in a spirit of common agreement, mutual support and open accountability.

Clearly, those who are in positions of trust and responsibility have a duty to work to this end. But institutional renewal usually comes about when an upward pressure created from below in the grass-roots coincides with a willingness to experiment and respond from those who are in positions of influence. Involvement in the committee structures of associations is one way of stimulating change or of being able to endorse it when it begins to happen. But this is not the only way. The creation of pockets of new life at the grass-roots level, in which experiments are attempted, can point the way and offer to the wider institution new possibilities for its own life when it is ready to take them up.

A first step from below in this process might be the commitment of pastoral leaders with a like-minded vision to meet together for purposes of friendship, support and correction. This may well happen in what are called fraternals, but sometimes the difficulties I have outlined above mean that these tend not to function as they should. It is a common experience for such occasions to be disappointing. They should be taken seriously because of the duty that all Christians have to seek for unity with those who are Christ's, but often they will fail to provide the warm and supportive friendship which pastors need. Some years ago I was one of a number of pastors in the north-west of England who entered into a commitment of friendship and mutual accountability. We would meet monthly to talk, laugh and pray and sometimes to weep together. It was the source of much strength in the middle of demanding and sometimes bruising ministries in which each of us was committed to bringing about change. We also found that quite inadvertently, we had stumbled on something for which others were looking and that we had become the catalyst for other such groups to arise in different parts of the country. It was evident then that, beneath the surface, pastoral leaders had many unmet needs that in some cases were causing acute personal pain. These needs still exist and if they are to be met initiatives must be taken to create many support groups or make existing fraternals more supportive. Here are shoots of new life growing up in the shelter of the old.

But this in itself does not constitute true association. As a first step, the coming together of pastoral leaders is essential but the second step must follow, namely the coming together of churches in a form of mutual support and accountability. The experiment in which I was involved never quite made this second step, for the simple reason that we had not at that time come to appreciate the theology of association. What happens then is that leaders come together for their personal benefit, but when they move on, they leave their churches in the same un- or semi-associated state in which they started, and this at a time when they might benefit more than at any other from support.

Association is the willing commitment of congregations to a process of mutual support, enrichment and correction. At this point the prophetic witness of the restoration movement may help in describing the content that such association can have. While deliberately avoiding the growth of new institutional forms of association, it draws our attention to the need for the building of relationships, the providing of opportunities for churches to gather together for inspiration and training, and the need for an articulated philosophy of mission and ministry which leads to the sharing of practical wisdom concerning the establishing of healthy churches. Each of these ingredients is essential and the absence of any one of them will mean that association is not achieved or becomes at most a stringing together of church connections with little purpose and effect.

In a Baptist context, the philosophy of mission and ministry would need to take account of how to enable churches to progress as harmoniously as possible through the change-processes in which many of them are involved. It would need to offer advice concerning the perennial problems which face

Baptist churches in search of renewal, yet these answers would need to be consistent with the values and principles which constitute Baptist identity. It would need to enable churches to make progress in a way in which some have failed to do for many years, stirring them back into life.

Understood in such terms, the renewal of association is needed and desired by many leaders and churches. I would not be so foolish as to imagine that everybody wants it, but those who do are following the same instinct which was followed by their Baptist forebears. How is this crucial second step to be achieved? I suggest three lines of thought, each of which may possibly be combined with either of the other two.

(1) It could be achieved by a number of churches in the same region or the same existing association resolving to come together to forge links. This may happen in the wake of what I have described in step one. The crucial point which marks the beginning of this new development occurs when churches decide *as churches* to seek for association. This would require not only the commitment of the leader or leaders but of the church as a whole and this in turn implies that the church understands, or can be brought to understand, the meaning of association. Such a decision may be taken after a time of growing together with others through joint gatherings and the like. Or it might be that the church commits itself to several years of exploration. The decision would need to be supported by purposeful co-operative ventures, to provide content for the theory, and by the investment of the necessary resources. But once several congregations started to achieve authentic fellowship, the renewal of the wider association structures could begin, as others were drawn in.

(2) This second step could also be achieved between churches drawn from a wider area transcending existing regional and association groupings. This widens the field of possibilities and is particularly helpful for churches which find there are no like-minded churches in their own vicinity. Given the speed of communications and the ease of travel in today's society, we are no longer limited by geography as once we

were. There is no reason therefore why new patterns which surpass existing structures might not be developed. It might be worth remembering that Baptist history gives evidence of such new initiatives in association, the most startling being the establishing by Dan Taylor, at the end of the eighteenth century, of a national 'connexion' of churches. Following this model, churches in different parts of the country who none the less share a common vision might come together in meaningful association and might contribute towards the re-discovery among Baptists generally of true association.

(3) A third line of thought expands the horizon even further. It might be possible to develop forms of association between Baptist churches inside the existing structures and new churches which are baptist in theology and practice and which are not in a denomination.

A number of comments are valid here. Existing reality indicates that many Baptist churches already have strong links with like-minded new churches. It is increasingly the case that many new churches have moved, or are moving, decisively away from authoritarian forms of church life which they once espoused. Furthermore, the prevailing mood in large sections of this movement (which is diverse and difficult to generalise about) is no longer separatist, but concerned to make common cause with other churches and to merge into the mainstream without necessarily applying for membership in any existing denomination.

Taken together with the changes that have been taking place in Baptist churches, this means that large numbers of Baptist or baptistic churches are within a whisker of each other in theology and practice. This opens up the possibility of churches coming together in association not only across regional barriers but across denominational ones in a form of affirming coalition between churches which share the same conviction concerning the believers' church.

Furthermore, because the new churches have themselves experimented with forms of association with various degrees of success, accumulating a maturity and a wisdom in this area, they might be able to infuse into many Baptist churches what they have learned. Conversely, Baptist churches, who come with a sense of historical perspective and with traditions of expository ministry and order, may impart to many new churches a sense of being rooted in history which otherwise would take them years to acquire. Both would acquire new networks and possibilities which would be immensely enriching.

What is being suggested here is only the equivalent of what is happening between Baptists and other historic denominations. The emphasis in the interchurch process is on a pilgrimage expressed through covenants in local ecumenical ventures. Some Baptist churches will be experimenting as a result of this with new forms of association across the historic denominational divides, and I have no quarrel with this. But the same logic should cause us to look also in other directions, towards churches which are newer in origin.

This chapter is almost complete. In it I have attempted to lay bare the meaning of association, to reflect upon its current practice and to suggest ways towards the renewing of association in the context of our time. I am arguing for the renewing of genuine association between the churches of the existing Baptist groupings, and beyond them with those of like mind. There is more to be said in the chapter which follows. I am advocating this because it is necessary. It is necessary for the sake of 'bodying forth' Jesus Christ the Lord, invisible but made visible through his people. It is also necessary for the sake of our well-being, that we may be upheld, supported, corrected and enriched in the churches as we pursue our pilgrimage.

There are encouraging signs that a new solidarity is on its way as associations engage increasingly in church-planting. Serious and systematic attempts are being made to reform existing patterns and increase their effectiveness in the life of the churches they serve. Experiments bringing folk together in ways different from the traditional assemblies are proving uniformly successful. These are signs of what could easily be.

But this is only a part. We must also have in view two wider objectives.

First, there is the renewal of the Baptist denomination. This will be achieved as, from the bottom up, a new solidarity and fellowship is realised among the churches, and as the leaders of the denomination encourage and increase this impetus. Once begun, this will become unstoppable and will produce from itself and draw into itself those men and women who will lead the institutional forms of our life to serve the mission of the church of God more effectively. Beyond this there is a more distant horizon, which includes the whole church throughout the world moving to a hoped-for future time when it is holy, catholic, apostolic and one. The way we hasten the coming of that day is by learning to relate organically in Christ to the parts of the body which are nearest to us and where unity is most likely to be forged. Yet our concern is not only for the part, but for the whole through the part. It is this universal perspective with which we are ultimately concerned, and with the world in which the church is called to bear its testimony, in word and life, to Jesus Christ.

6

Reforming the Powers that Be

If you have survived this far into the book, you will inevitably
have noticed that I regard institutions as a mixed blessing. On
the one hand, if the church is to live and witness in a given
community it needs to establish institutions or organisations
to advance its projects. Institutional forms are simply inevitable. On the other hand, there is a tendency for such institutions to become detached from the end in view, to develop a
life of their own and to become self-important. They always
risk becoming arenas for vested interests and illegitimate self-
advancement. I would much prefer it, then, if the church of
Christ held such forms as loosely as possible, concentrated on
people and relationships and minimised the distorting effect.

The down-side of institutions is that they become concerned to protect themselves. They often attract the kind of
person who will avoid being radical, necessitate the learning
of bureaucratic rather than relational and spiritual qualities,
engage in competition with other institutions, demand finance
for their own needs and use people for their own ends. Most
of all, they breed power games, the aim of which is to bend
the energies of the system in one direction or another. If it be
objected that none of this is necessarily the case, my response
is that institutions gravitate in these directions and it takes

great presence of mind and strength of purpose to have it otherwise. Happily, there are those who arise from time to time who have these qualities and produce reform.

This brings us to the up-side of institutional life. Once properly directed, they are able to achieve more good than might be achieved by a myriad of individuals working separately. They can lend credibility and act as a platform for people with something good to say. They can resource and enable fruitful activity. They can provide a context and a platform for the use of exceptional gifts. They can enable people to rise to the full stature of their abilities by investing confidence and expectations in them and by placing them at the centre of the flow of events. But to do this they must be captured and held for the kingdom, that is, bent to the service of the saving work of God in the world.

In this chapter I am concerned with one major institution, the Baptist Union of Great Britain, which, despite its name, mainly serves churches in England and some in Wales. This may sound like a big switch-off to some readers, particularly those who are reading this book for what it says about Baptist values rather than about Baptist denominational affairs. I dare to believe that even in this chapter such readers might find something of value. I make no apology for addressing this subject. It is of practical importance to many thousands of people. It reflects the belief that all things, visible and invisible, are called to bow the knee to Jesus Christ, and this involves the organisational life of the human race in which the church is the first-fruits of redemption.

Furthermore, changes are afoot, to which we have already referred, which make the final decade of the twentieth century a possible season of progressive and startling change for the Baptist Union. The catalyst of the removal of Union offices, from an outmoded Edwardian building in central London to newly built, high tech premises in Didcot, could work wonders as we approach not only the next century but the next millennium. Change and reform are more likely now than they have been for decades and the language of reform needs to be upon our lips and in our hearts. Following the lines of thought already developed, my hope is now to apply them to the denominational structures of the Union. To do this we need to make an historical detour so that we understand where we have come from.

The Baptist Union is a relative newcomer in Baptist terms. From the beginning British Baptists have shared a common life in associations. It was two hundred years later that a society was formed, in 1813, with the object of providing a national forum which would join ministers, churches and associations together more closely. The Baptist Union should be dated from this time. Its early objects included the exciting of brotherly love and co-operation between ministers and churches, and support for missions through the Baptist Missionary Society which was formed in 1792.

The early Union was evangelical and Calvinist in theology. In the course of the nineteenth century, the two Baptist denominations which had existed since the early part of the seventeenth century, although with changes and detours en route, grew steadily together. The Particular Baptists (Calvinists) and the General Baptists (Arminians) were increasingly making common cause and this led to the amalgamation of the Baptist Union with the New Connexion of General Baptists in 1891. It is from this time that the Union as an inclusive evangelical body such as we now know it has existed.

In the early decades of the twentieth century, under the leadership of Dr J.H. Shakespeare, the central institutional development of the Union went ahead by leaps and bounds. This period corresponded with the height of Baptist numerical strength at a time when one in two of the population was connected with nonconformity. Baptist self-confidence and political influence were at their height. Nearly all of the features of Baptist institutional life were added at this time, including the new headquarters building, central development funds and area superintendents. If the Baptist Union has known a golden age, this was it. Since then, the general decline common to organised Christian denominations in this country has taken its toll.

This brief sketch serves as a basis for raising certain questions about the Union which, expressed or unexpressed, have sapped something of its life during its brief history. For clarity's sake we shall number them.

(1) There have been persistent questions about the theological commitment of the Union and about its tolerance of interpretations of the gospel which appear to be unorthodox. It needs to be admitted that this is a complex area, since two Baptist principles are in danger of coming into collision. Baptists are orthodox Christians and stand in the evangelical tradition of the Reformation. In their historic confessions they have sought to turn away criticisms by showing that they adhere to historic Christian beliefs, while differing in the doctrines of the church and baptism from other Christians. At the same time they have strongly asserted freedom of conscience and the autonomy of the local church, and have rejected the imposition or enforcement of religious beliefs in credal form in favour of freedom of thought and of theological enquiry.

The problem occurs when free theological enquiry is seen to carry people beyond the bounds of orthodox and evangelical faith. When this happens, should those concerned be encouraged in their freedom or disciplined because of their unorthodoxy? How inclusive is the Baptist Union able to be before it betrays itself and its faith? As a union of Calvinists and Arminians it plainly committed itself to a range of theological diversity, but only within limits that may be recognised as evangelical. And yet who is to define what is meant by evangelical?

Questions such as these have been around for many years and were given impetus by the Down Grade Controversy in 1887–8, a lacerating dispute which cast a shadow over the Union for years to come. Its tangled threads are still difficult to unravel. The controversy was initiated by the most distinguished and influential Baptist of the nineteenth century,

C.H. Spurgeon, who believed he detected in the ranks the creeping influence of modernism and universalism. He feared that an apostasy from evangelical truth was imminent, such as had grievously debilitated Baptists in the eighteenth century and led many off into Unitarianism. The majority opinion in the Union was not favourable to Spurgeon and the eventual outcome was that he resigned from its ranks, being followed in this by others. As it happened, opinion was divided even among his own friends, family and students, and remains divided to this day.

It seems in retrospect that two things were happening in the theological climate of the times which became confused. One was that, in some circles, unorthodox views were indeed being expressed which represented a departure from evangelical faith. The other was that evangelical believers were undergoing a legitimate process of reflection, in the light of advancing knowledge, which was leading to less rigid categories of thought in certain areas. The former is rightly to be identified and resisted, because it goes beyond the limits of what may legitimately be called Baptist. The latter, however, must be regarded as a necessary and responsible task, the alternative to which is the defensive repetition of the theology of a previous age. This is in no way a betrayal, but a re-appropriation of evangelical truth in a new context. To discern between these two activities would appear to be crucial.

The Down Grade Controversy left a suspicion about the commitment of the Union, which from that time onwards has seen examples of churches seceding and fellowshipping elsewhere. Fuel was added to this particular fire in 1971, when a respected college principal gave an address at the Baptist Union Assembly in London in which he appeared to question the doctrines of the Incarnation and of the deity of Christ. Once more questions were raised about orthodoxy and legitimate freedom. A major catastrophe was narrowly averted by an overwhelmingly supported motion during the following year's Assembly re-affirming the Union's commitment to christological orthodoxy.

Yet rightly or wrongly, the common judgement persists that the establishment of the Union is at best half-hearted in its evangelical commitment and at worst theologically liberal. This is one of the perceptions which must be remedied. For the moment, let it be said that a voluntary Christian body can only function harmoniously and constructively if it does so on the basis of theological agreement.

(2) A further area of questioning which may be detected concerns a suspicion of the centralising tendencies of the Union. The twentieth century has seen the development of a denominational hierarchy in a way which would have been unthinkable in previous centuries. Sociologists of religion might point out that, as they evolve, denominations have a tendency to compensate for loosened theological bonds by tightening up elsewhere. Official control is intensified, professionalism emphasised, academic and social respectability sought. This is the story of Baptists in the early twentieth century. From being a network of independently-minded churches and associations, the Baptists have developed for themselves centralised denominational agencies controlling and dispensing considerable sums of money.

With this have gone the inevitable paraphernalia—a central council appointed by election, with power to co-opt and to appoint committees dealing with all manner of issues, and internal legislation governing the work of the organisation as a whole. Add to this a secretariat and allied departments and a considerable organisation emerges. All of this is a way of saying that the Union has developed bureaucratic characteristics and that bureaucracy and spiritual renewal are potentially unsympathetic to one another. For good or ill we have moved some way from the covenant community with which we began.

It is not surprising that the process of centralisation has created suspicion. Human beings do well to cultivate a healthy scepticism towards any powerful structure, not least those which are ecclesiastical. From time to time, a call goes out for us to remember that the Baptist Union is the churches which belong to it: 'You are the Baptist Union!' Yet this call is not altogether realistic. The fact is that once a central, organised institution has developed, it becomes something in its own right, with a momentum, a 'personality' and a power of its own. The whole is always greater than the sum of the parts. The Baptist Union may be the churches, but it is also something over against, and distinguishable from, the churches.

Moreover, having charted a centralising and standardising course, voices are sometimes raised advocating that we continue in this direction. The idea of a central salary-structure for the payment of ministers is one suggestion. An argument could be made for this in terms of sharing together in ministry and mission, but it would entail a different theological rationale from the congregational theology with which we began. A precedent for the continuation of the move to the centre is available to us in the history of Congregational churches. Having begun with an understanding of the autonomy of the local church almost identical to our own, they first became the Congregational Union, then the Congregational Church and currently (for most of them) the United Reformed Church. Each step in this direction took them further away from the insights into the nature of the church with which they began.

Reviewing the history of the Baptist Union in the early twentieth century reveals a trajectory towards the centre which would have led to the Baptist Church. Soon I shall argue that this whole movement was ill-conceived and that for the future a new emphasis on decentralisation, already in some respects evident, should be encouraged. First, however, a theological point must be made.

(3) The Baptist Union is an organisation which badly needs a theological overhaul. This is the most serious criticism that I have to make of it. The justification for the Baptist Union is that it is an expression of the catholic nature of the church and of the fact that each church must take its place responsibly within the wider fellowship of churches. This is an imperative and cannot be denied. The question concerns how this is best

done and whether along the way we have taken some wrong turns. Behind the development of the Union were legitimate instincts and a commendable concern for brotherly and sisterly love. There were also practical concerns, which had to do with the support of the Baptist Missionary Society. An element of expediency and practical necessity was involved, which is not of itself wrong but may not be governed by proper theological insights.

But, and here is the concern, the development of the Union was also shaped by a process of accommodation to the pattern of the established church which operated with a markedly different concept of what the church is. That this was happening should not surprise us. After the great numerical growth, social advances and political emancipation of the nineteenth century, Baptists at the turn of the century were self-confident and optimistic. They had grown in respectability and influence and were likely therefore to cast off the traditions of dissent and nonconformity and to become 'like the nations' in their aspirations and methods. It is my contention that this led to a wrong turn in a centralising direction which now needs to be remedied by a process of reform.

In 1961, the Baptist Union published a document entitled *The Doctrine of the Ministry*, in which the authors were clearly conscious of the need to justify in theological terms the existence of Baptist organisations. They recognised that the New Testament bore witness to only two dimensions of the church, the local and the universal, but felt that the Baptist Union could be justified as an expression of larger corporate life and responsibility among Baptists consistent with this picture. They then added:

It does not mean, however, that structures of organisation are unalterable. The organisation of the local church, of the Association, of the Baptist Union and the Baptist Missionary Society must always be subject to the changing situations of Christian witness, and to growing insight into the nature of the church and its ministry. The unchanging pattern for the life of the church is given in Jesus Christ.

I am particularly concerned here with the words 'subject...to growing insight into the nature of the church and its ministry'. What is needed for the Baptist Union is once more a recovery and re-appropriation of Baptist insights, leading to reform.

(4) A further area in which confidence in the Baptist Union has been weakened is the ecumenical, although the issues here are perhaps more difficult than might first be imagined, since those who are unenthusiastic about ecumenism differ concerning their reasons.

There are those who are hostile to ecumenism in principle, since it smells to them of betraying the truth. Beneath this statement lie some huge gulfs concerning the nature of truth and the status of others in the kingdom of God who confess Christ but not with the same qualifications as we do. There are others who support a limited ecumenism within a spectrum of theological positions believed to be acceptable. The discussion here would involve the legitimate limits to the spectrum. There are yet others who are for an ecumenical vision in principle, but believe that the search for it via the institutional pathway, that is to say ecumenical organisational structures, is ill-advised.

While acknowledging the position of those who are concerned about the content of our confession, I count myself among those who believe it to be a Christian duty to search for a true unity with all those who are Christ's. Yet the current approach seems to me to be in danger of already conceding that the church is institution and that the search for unity is an institutional search. What may well happen, therefore, is the development of more bureaucracy and ecumenical elites. This danger is acknowledged by the Swanwick Declaration of 1987, which sought to revive the ecumenical dialogue by transmuting the old institution of the British Council of Churches into a process of interchurch pilgrimage.

This shift in itself is welcome but needs to be taken further. Because the church is people gathered by the Spirit, the unity of the church is only going to be achieved by the forging of friendships between Christian people in the Spirit. Though this is more difficult than setting up new organisations which produce the impression of achievement, it is where the focus should be. My fear is that Baptist Christians may make an implicit and unwitting surrender of their theological insight by accommodating to institutional models of the church. As I also see this as a criticism of the way the Baptist Union developed, it may be gathered that I discern a major problem here.

What I wish to argue for is a more consistently Baptist understanding of the church in the domestic and external affairs of the Baptist Union, which could then be reflected in our ecumenical witness. This ought to lead to new ways of doing things, which are determined neither by expediency alone nor by accommodation to others, but by our own values and principles. Without imagining that we are anywhere else than at the beginning of this task, I wish now to advance some ideas which might act as an invitation to conversation. How may the Baptist Union be changed so as to receive the confidence of the churches and to be an effective vehicle of mission for today?

Of first importance is the need for it to recover explicitly its evangelical identity. Baptists are evangelical Christians or they are nothing. The point has already been made that evangelical faith is an indispensable element in Baptist history and identity. Here it needs to be emphasised because the Union as a body will only command the full-hearted support of the churches if it is convincing on this point. It is for this reason that the helpful debates in recent years about Baptist identity lead on inevitably to the further debate about what it means to be evangelical. Both these debates are related to the further question of whether there are limits to theological opinion acceptable in the Union. How do we work through these issues in a healthy manner?

My intention is to argue that Baptists need to re-appropriate the word 'evangelical', use it self-consciously of themselves and be true to it in theology and in practice. To do this it must be understood as a word which describes a theological tradition rather than a party. Certain words develop in the course of time a secondary meaning referring to a party and then fall upon hard times because people decline to see themselves in party terms and distance themselves from the word. The word 'evangelical' is like this and needs to be re-owned— but this must be done honestly and with regard to its substance.

In substance it refers to a stream of faith which has its origin in the New Testament and came to fresh expression in the Reformation. Along with the orthodox doctrines of the faith, it affirms the priority of Scripture, of grace and of faith. Of Scripture, because it believes there is to be found there a word which has priority as an authority for faith and conduct over all other authorities, both in the church and outside it. We are bound to hear it and live by it. Of grace, because it believes that the salvation of undeserving sinners is not self-achieved but is given by a God who, through Christ and in Christ-like love, accepts us as his children. From first to last, salvation is of God. Of faith, because it affirms that salvation comes to us through conversion leading to personal trust in Christ, of which, for Baptists, baptism is the sign. To be persuaded of these truths is to be evangelical.

Yet there is room for diversity in the midst of common conviction, and attempts to set up particular touchstones of evangelicalism, such as specific theories of the Atonement or inspiration, should be resisted. Most importantly, diversity may be found around the question of the priority of Scripture. The affirmation of this leaves room for differences in the way in which the inspiration of Scripture is understood and what it is held to imply. There are even more questions about the way in which it is to be interpreted. But such diversity has a common point of origin in the intention to submit to the word of God in Scripture.

It is entirely possible to conceive of the Baptist Union as a coalition of conservative, liberal and radical evangelicals seeking to live faithfully under the word of God. In fact, it becomes increasingly obvious that evangelicalism, understood in broader terms than the Baptist world, is itself just such a coalition. But to move outside the evangelical tradition, with its commitment to decisive biblical authority, is to move beyond what may with integrity be termed 'Baptist'.

For the sake of their church life, Baptists need to see themselves self-consciously as evangelical Christians and to affirm their commitment. Within this framework there is considerable freedom for theological opinion and debate—the more the better, since this is one way in which we may serve each other. Yet there is a logical limit to the degree to which someone who wishes to be called a Baptist may diverge from the tradition. Within the framework of a democratic society, in which British Baptists live and which they support, there is freedom of opinion and all people may hold their convictions. But integrity has its own demands and membership of a confessional body should not be treated cynically. The theological integrity of a movement will best be maintained by the personal integrity of those within its ranks who are seeking for truth. Those who depart from certain beliefs should no longer pretend that they hold them but do the honest thing and seek a more congenial home. This is the best form of theological discipline to encourage, a self-regulating one.

In second place I wish to argue that the word 'reformation' should be once more on our lips when we think about the Baptist Union. The time for action is right, the thinking needs to be done and constructive moves initiated or, where reform is already in process, supported. The final decade of the twentieth century should be marked by adventurous change controlled by a sound theology and a commitment to relevance.

The weakest part of the Baptist doctrine of the church concerns its national denominational structures. In our understanding of the covenant community of believers we are at our strongest, and in the concept of association a useful tool has been developed for relating the local churches to each other in accountability and action. But our national structures detract from these strengths in two ways. Theologically, we are stretching the concept of association to make the Union an association of associations. Relationally, we are in danger of depriving it of any meaning by putting the Union beyond the effective reach of the local churches which it is supposed to serve and to which it is accountable.

These two points belong together, since I would argue that once association is stretched this far it ceases to be meaningful. It may only be operated on the basis of a bureaucratic (and therefore distant) model rather than on a relational one. The whole has become an organisation rather than an organism and we are no longer dealing with the ideas with which we began. The institutional is in danger of eating up the relational.

In seeking for a better way, it seems wise to build highest where the foundations are at their strongest and only modestly where they are in question. This would mean pursuing the policy of decentralisation and thus reversing the trend observed in the early part of this century, since the strength of Baptist doctrine lies in its concept of the local church and then of churches in association. We have already discussed reasons for the decline in Baptist associations but omitted to mention the primary reason, which was their eclipse in proportion to the development of the Union. Once the Union began to assume many of the functions of the associations and to use them as channels of its own life, they were in danger of becoming little more than administrative units of the Union. This was a retreat from an important insight. Effective support can only be given when there is a relationship which enables it to happen.

The analogy still applies with the local church. While it remains a community bound by ties of fellowship and friendship, it may fulfil its function. Once it becomes merely a society it cannot. The present association structures leave much to be desired and are themselves in need of reform, but in practice they remain theologically, historically and practically the most viable vehicles for the expression of a corporate witness. Most importantly, because they are in psychological walking distance of the churches to which they are accountable, they are capable of being reformed more quickly.

In general terms, allowing for local variations, there are three levels of organised Baptist life outside the local church. There are districts, which are subdivisions of associations, associations themselves and the Union. In order for associations to be revitalised it would be necessary for a shift of emphasis to take place, with some of the existing functions of the Union being pushed out to the associations. This would create a downward pressure which would enhance their importance and therefore bring larger numbers of people from the grass-roots into active participation in association structures. At the same time, to modify, or even in some cases abolish, existing structures at district level (which are often ineffective) could create an upward pressure, by freeing people for participation at association level. In turn, this could create a demand for internal reform of the associations.

The essential elements of such reform would be institutional, representational and inspirational. Association structures which have often grown up piecemeal would need to be simplified extensively and move towards an organic emphasis upon relationships. To ensure that there is fair and adequate participation of all the churches, new approaches to representation would have to be discovered, bringing churches more fully and more easily into the decision-making process. The development of the spiritual life of the associations would necessitate a change in the pattern of open meetings towards a progressive, inspirational emphasis concerned with the spiritual health and progress of the churches.

The value and potential benefit of such gatherings should not be underestimated, and entirely new patterns could emerge, going far beyond the idea of 'annual meetings', as is already happening in some areas. It is essential to make the corporate life of an association both meaningful and eventful and to take it beyond the maintenance of the status quo into a concern for positive spiritual achievements. The revitalisation of association life could well lead to the emergence of new associations resulting from the dividing up of the old, found now to be too large, or even the coming into being of others which are completely new. These might well operate on different patterns of association, transcending the usual geographical borders. It might even be that the process I am describing would begin to make the Baptist family a natural home for new churches and their networks, as they themselves feel more intensely the need for wider and more deeply-rooted relational ties. If this were the case, the Baptist Union could be facing far more than small-scale increases in membership.

Encouraging the renewal of associations in the way I suggest could only take place at the cost of a form of self-denying ordinance from the Baptist Union. I believe this to be theologically desirable, so that corporate Baptist life is built at the point where the theology is strongest. It is also strategically necessary as a way of opening up the situation and pushing responsibility outwards. Several decisive steps could initiate this process.

First, the Union could invest money in providing for the associations an infrastructure adequate to cope with an enhanced role. This would involve new offices, equipment and personnel. Secondly, the Union could make a major financial shift whereby money currently gathered by the associations and passed on to the Union would be retained by the associations and administered by them. It would then be up to the associations to fund the Union by donating a proportion of this income to it, rather than up to the Union to finance the associations by returning money to them. This involves a shift of power away from the centre which will relativise the importance of the Union and strengthen that of the associations.

The association would then become directly responsible for

the support and supervision of aided churches within its ranks and for the provision of other resources in mission. Less well provided areas could be helped by the development of an equalisation fund to which associations could contribute. It is at this point that the rubber would hit the road and the decentralisation would become a reality.

A third essential step would involve the direct election and employment of area superintendents by the churches of their own area, rather than their being employed, as at present, by the Baptist Union. This is more in keeping with Baptist church order since, if the association is understood as a parallel to the fellowship of the local church, it would mirror the accepted practice of local churches in calling and employing their own staff. The churches of each association, or of groups of associations acting together according to size, should appoint their own superintendents. The Union has already taken a decisive step in this direction by ensuring that their appointment, although formally by the Union through its Council, is nevertheless at the recommendation of a group that is heavily weighted in favour of the association. My suggestion follows the logic of this trend. Within the constraints of their resources, it would mean that associations could make as many appointments as they wished and could develop patterns of ministry which seemed appropriate for their situation.

Depending on one's perspective, the above reforms would either deprive the Baptist Union of a meaningful role or confirm it in making its true contribution. There is no doubt that it would take immense courage to make these steps. They would have the effect of concentrating the Union machinery into being what it has been intended to be all along, a resource agency existing to serve the life of the associations and of the churches but relying only on the quality of its work and the depth of its influence to do so. In this area there is a great deal to do, but the Union would have to make the necessary legal and constitutional changes to adapt.

I would advocate here the abolition of the annual Assembly

as a legislative body composed of various types of personal, ex officio and representative memberships. Such a function could be exercised in a different fashion, either through extraordinary meetings called when appropriate or by an increased use of postal votes. The existing Baptist Union Council, suitably reconstituted, would become the body directly responsible for the national resource agency. To ensure its truly representative nature, it would need to be composed of those elected by the associations (a larger number than at present) with a limited number of ex officio appointments. The place of co-opted members is debatable but it ought to be possible to co-opt folk to the Council in a consultative, rather than a voting, capacity. The object of these reforms would be to increase the level of direct accountability to the churches served.

The tasks of the Union could then be developed as follows:

(1) The Union would provide opportunities for Baptist Christians to gather on a national basis for inspiration, communication, instruction and deliberation. Shorn of legislative tasks, the gatherings of the Union could be more directly related to the spiritual aims of Baptist Christians and could break out of the restricted patterns which now exist. Events such as Spring Harvest have shown what is possible and it is a sobering thought that far more Baptists attend these than would ever think of turning up to the Union Assembly. Such occasions could give immense opportunities for the development of church members and their leaders and could be significant in the life of the nation. In addition, the Union could offer specialist conferences and might consider acquiring for that purpose a suitable profit-making conference centre, which would also serve the life of the associations in general. In determining what is necessary, the Union would act in consultation with the associations it exists to serve.

(2) The Union would resource the processes of consultation and communication between the associations. The existing structure of committees appointed by the Council and composed of its members could be replaced by working groups directly appointed from the associations to deal with the vital

areas of national and common concern. The most important of these would be the gathering of superintendents from the associations whose numbers would rise as existing areas divided and new associations formed. Interchurch affairs, mission and evangelism, ministerial recognition, education, political affairs and the like could all be represented, by appointment from the associations and serviced by the Union on behalf of the associations in general. The Union would need to employ the staff to fulfil these tasks and to act as effective spokespersons for Baptist Christians. The need for a national system of ministerial accreditation, one of the most important of all the services offered by the Union, would be fulfilled in this way.

(3) The Union would provide encouragement and resources for the provision of suitable, professionally produced literature at all levels from the profoundly theological to the popular. This is currently a woefully neglected area and has contributed not a little to the ignorance among Baptists about their own theology. It may be that publication work could be carried on by negotiating an understanding with an existing publishing house rather than by starting from scratch. In any event, new developments in desktop publishing have opened up the field for cheaper publishing very considerably. A part of this task would be the production of news publications of which we could be justly proud. Major improvements in our present standards could be achieved by moving to a monthly, rather than a weekly, publication. The United Reformed Church made such a change some years ago, and now publishes an excellent monthly called *Reform*, as did the Assemblies of God, who publish *Redemption*. Could we not do the same and call it *Freedom*? The publications of the Union must be second-to-none in anticipating what is needed and making it available.

(4) A further area concerns the legal, technical and financial resourcing which is made available through the Union and which will always be necessary. To this role could be added the opening of new initiatives which will benefit Baptist Chris-

tians. For instance, the development of credit unions making low-interest loans available would be of enormous help to pastors who have to purchase their own cars and a practical benefit to many church members. The setting of standards for the common practice of the churches fits into this category and could be beneficial not only in the setting of *minimum* salary levels and travelling expenses but in going beyond this to establish a *recommended* salary level (which is more than minimum). Advice would be helpful in other areas where practices are whimsical rather than thoughtful, such as the payment of fees.

(5) A final and most important task on which we might touch concerns the unique position that such an agency is in, first of all to identify the forms of ministry and mission which are needed for today and then to encourage associations, churches and pastors to take up the challenges which become clear. Some of these needs might be met by the Union itself in encouraging and resourcing the development of special ministries, particularly in the area of evangelism. Denominational leaders should be seen first and foremost as people of God, spiritual leaders with a strategic ministry to offer to the church for its upbuilding in faith and mission.

The possibilities outlined here make it plain that there is much good work that a national resource agency can do. Whether what I have described here is still best called 'the Baptist Union' is debatable, but then, among the other changes I advocate is a change of name just to round things off and symbolise the shift in operations. The word 'Union' is not appropriate because it paves the way for 'Church'. A more accurate description of what ought to be would be a 'National Association of Baptist Churches' or perhaps, following the American Baptist Convention, which has renamed itself 'American Baptist Churches', it ought to be 'English (or British?) Baptist Churches'.

It seems to me that the shift of direction I have advocated would make the Baptist Union serve the same function in national terms that the Baptist Missionary Society does internationally. It would clarify its role as an agency which exists to serve the churches in their work of mission and to provide expertise of which the local church is not capable on its own. It offers knowledge, wisdom, resources and contacts which the local church has little hope of achieving alone.

In closing this chapter it is worth pointing out that the reforming shifts suggested in it are directly paralleled by what is happening all over the world, and not least in our own country, in business and political terms. We might take a nationalised industry as an example. After the last war nationalisation took into public ownership industries which previously had been run badly, unevenly or by vested interests which had little concern for their workforce. Nationalisation served to upgrade many industries by bringing in government investment, laying down minimum standards and being concerned for those who created the wealth by their labour. Yet the tendency of nationalised industries to become bureaucratic and unresponsive and to develop new forms of vested interest not in the interest of the consumer led in time to a need to stop the centralising trend and to devolve power. In the 1980s this was done by massive privatisation. Some think (me included) that new forms of common ownership and co-operative developments would have served everybody's interest better. At any rate, something needed to be done to increase flexibility and responsiveness to the needs the industries were created to serve.

It is a comparable shift that is needed in the Baptist Union, and for similar reasons. The intention is genuinely to return the Union to the people and to put it within the common ownership of the local churches. Even if the specific proposals of this chapter do not always commend themselves in detail, they are at least an invitation to conversation and the closing years of this millennium need to witness a debate in which the language of adventurous reform should be widely spoken and heard.

The current Baptist scene indicates that the desire to move

in a decentralising direction is already well-rooted among many leading Baptists. It would not be fair to give the impression that the basic burden of this chapter is novel or unheard of. Encouraging signs of the desire to serve and to mobilise, rather than to control or restrict, are present already. But reform is demanding and requires for its implementation an atmosphere of responsive welcome. Where this attitude is abroad, the possibilities increase. Effective reform of complex structures requires far more detailed analysis of existing reality and possible alternatives than is possible in a chapter. A significant initiative in Baptist circles would be the appointing of a commission to examine the situation, identify the principles involved and set the guidelines for progressive institutional change. The Baptist Union needs to be stimulated into being the proactive and visionary body that its member churches require it to be.

7

The Case for Baptist Bishops

When I was a young believer I fondly imagined that what made Baptists different from anybody else was that they do not believe in bishops. I recall being present on one occasion when a visiting Baptist area superintendent was introduced as 'the nearest thing Baptists have to a bishop'. Even such an oblique and obviously true statement sounded offensive to me at the time. I was learning then to be a defender of congregational autonomy and believed bishops to be the kind of persons from whom it needed to be defended! I learned in time that things were not that simple and, to my surprise, a good case for bishops could be made.

A number of things helped to change my mind. One was that leadership in the church was always meant to be shared and not solitary. It always seemed pretty clear from reading the New Testament that leadership within the congregation was meant to be plural. The model that I saw around me, and was more or less taken for granted in my vocational training, never did strike me as authentic. That ministers should be solely responsible for the oversight of their churches seemed odd. It was even odder that their singular status was marked by the wearing on occasion of a clerical collar (Lord preserve us!), a gown and (at baptisms) huge wellingtons, presumably to add dignity to the occasion!

This was not and is not the model for ministry which I saw in the New Testament. Rather, I perceived there a sharing of leadership between those whose ministries were different but complementary, which strengthened the church by giving it security and solidarity. The development of such patterns within local churches has now become commonplace and its significance for the wider church needs to be appreciated. In my own work the theory was confirmed by the practice, as I realised swiftly that I needed as much help as I could get. Appreciation of my need for colleagues from within the local church was followed by the realisation that in addition I needed counsellors from outside it. I needed help in restoring the flagging energy, sorting out the tangled emotions, clarifying the future direction and, occasionally, resolving contentious issues. I began to perceive something which seems to be taken for granted in other parts of the church, and indeed in any other caring profession—that I needed oversight and supervision, or to give it another term, bishoping. Baptists have preferred, on the whole, a system of rugged individualism to see them through.

My conversion was completed when I came into touch with the restoration movement. Here were people who were practising some of the things that I was convinced from Scripture and experience to be right. They were operating shared leaderships, practising association and developing the gifts of the body of Christ, and to all of this I was aspiring. But there was an element that was completely new to me and which caused serious questioning, that is, the ministry of 'apostles'. Without ever buying into it in the form in which it was being offered, this ministry nevertheless helped me to see that the office of bishop which I had instinctively rejected was the kind which existed in the Church of England, as I then understood it. But I began to realise that there were other ways of fulfilling the role of a bishop. They were not to do with pomp and circumstance, with rings on the finger and overtones of lordship (and even this is a caricature and does not take account of the best in Anglicanism), but with senior and experienced pastors who had genuine spiritual authority caring for other pastors and their churches because their ministry was desired and accepted.

In time I became aware of distinctions in the restoration movement concerning styles of apostleship and that whereas some inclined towards authority-conscious modes of thinking, others very definitely saw that the apostolic function was not to dominate the local church but to serve it in its own attempts to discern God's will and be faithful to it and to enhance, rather than remove, its freedom. It was possible then to contemplate a bishoping role which fully respected the autonomy of the local church, enhanced freedom of conscience and understood authority in Christ-like terms as the authority of love and wise counsel, not of hierarchical power. In these terms, such a role, while not necessary for the well-being of the church in an essential way, was indeed necessary for its well-being in a practical way.

There is a further difference from more traditional forms of episcopacy. The concept of a historic episcopate emphasises historical continuity in the church from the time of the first apostles. The channels of this continuity are the consecrated bishops by whose authority the affairs of the church are regularised. The bishop has therefore an essential role in the maintenance of the true church. Free church believers have rejected this approach and seen the continuity of the church in terms of its faithfulness to apostolic life and doctrine. A church may then be outside the established order but none the less truly a church because of the living presence of Christ in its midst, made known in faithful teaching and the ordinances.

An alternative to the historic approach is what may be called a functional episcopacy, concerned above all with providing for the church forms of ministry which enable it to fulfil itself in the service of God. My interest in this chapter is in pursuing this line of thought and in exploring how the life of the gathered church may be enriched by the recognition that

God has provided bishoping ministries for his people. To do this I need first of all to construct a case for the role itself and then to discuss what relevance this has for Baptist Christians.

The case from the New Testament

The case begins with a return to New Testament foundations. At this point we must examine the terms we have been using without, so far, much definition. We must also say something about the New Testament itself. While making every attempt to listen to it carefully, we do not imagine that it contains a rigid blueprint for the church that may be followed in every culture at every time. There are those who have approached it in this way and many Anabaptists and Baptists have been among them. The more the New Testament is studied, the more obvious it becomes that the early Christians showed great flexibility in adapting themselves to the cultures in which they were set. In this they set us an example. It is of prime importance to find how we may best operate for the sake of the gospel in our present age and to adapt our church structures accordingly. It is not wrong for the church to reflect the sociological patterns of its society, although sometimes it will also need to challenge them.

To guide us there is an overall theology of the church which may be gathered from the New Testament as a whole and there is the example of the early church as to how it was put into practice in their day and culture. We may learn from these sources as we engage in conversation with the New Testament and with our own situation. Perhaps we may describe this as 'principled flexibility'. Adaptability is evident in the variety of the terms which are used for leadership roles in the New Testament church. It is not clear exactly what some of these roles involved and we must be careful not to read back into the text our preconceived ideas.

For instance, the word 'deacon' conjures up pretty definite images for most Baptists. The deacon is often described as the 'nuts and bolts' person who does all the ordinary jobs about the church premises and lets the pastor and/or elders get on with the spiritual tasks. Whatever else we are unsure of, we can be sure that in the New Testament this is not what a deacon was. The church had no premises in those days and deacons exercised a pastoral role. Yet we are apt to read back our stereotypes into the biblical words.

So it is with the word 'bishop'. In the New Testament two words are used interchangeably. The word *episkopos* (from which 'bishop' is derived) was drawn from the Greek word and means 'one who oversees'. The word *presbuteros* (from which we get 'presbyter') comes from Jewish circles and refers to an older person. Both words were used in general terms to refer to officers of society and in Acts 20:17 and 28 both are used in reference to the same groups of church leaders, showing that they amount to the same thing. Strictly speaking then, 'bishop' is just another word for an elder within the church.

The real issue concerns the word 'apostle' and we should be grateful that renewed attention has been given to this word recently. The Catholic tradition has always seen the need for the continuation of the apostolic ministry in some form and it happens that from among the available terms in the New Testament, 'bishop' is the one that came to be applied to those who were seen as the successors of the first apostles. The use of the word 'apostle' today can be confusing and can sound like a claim to unique authority and status, because of the unrepeatable position of the original twelve apostles. For this reason the post-apostolic church was probably wise to avoid it in general use and the same policy might be adopted today.

The twelve apostles were an unrepeatable group because they were witnesses to the resurrection of Jesus (Acts 1:21–22) and this inevitably made them unique. Yet the evidence of the New Testament suggests that 'apostle' was used more broadly than simply of the Twelve. James (1 Cor 15:7), Barnabas (Acts 14:4, 14; 1 Cor 9:5–6), Silas (1 Thess 2:7), Timothy (1 Thess 2:6–7), Andronicus and Junia (Rom 16:7) are all mentioned as apostles, even though they did not belong to the original twelve.

What emerges is a picture of two related groups. The first is a group of twelve who had been with Christ from the beginning and who were witnesses of the resurrection and therefore able to be the authoritative interpreters of the faith. The second is a wider group fulfilling important evangelistic, missionary and overseeing functions within the church. They were recognised as commissioned to plant and nurture churches. Paul may be seen as making a bridge between the two types. While the first group was closed and unrepeatable, the second was open and there is no reason to imagine that it does not remain open. In this fact there is a biblical foundation for apostolic forms of ministry functioning translocally, that is, with responsibilities across a number of churches and not only in one.

For the believer in the gathered church there is also a challenge to come to terms with an understanding of Christian ministry which recognises this dimension and sees its relevance to the present. The New Testament both makes it permissible to contemplate a broader concept of ministry than that commonly espoused in Baptist circles and also requires a response from us in this area. In Ephesians 4:11 reference is made to a fivefold ministry which is given to the church by the ascended Lord and which includes apostles, prophets, evangelists, pastors and teachers.

It has commonly been assumed that some of these ministry functions have ceased since the apostolic age. Usually this is thought to be true of apostles and prophets, although Calvin also thought it true of evangelists. Yet the force of the passage itself would suggest otherwise. Such ministries are given to prepare the body of Christ for works of service 'until we all reach unity in the faith and in the knowledge of the Son of God and become mature, attaining to the whole measure of the fulness of Christ' (v12). In this word 'until' there is the clear suggestion that these ministries continue to be necessary until the reason for which they are given, attaining to the measure of Christ's fulness, is fulfilled. By anybody's standards, this did not happen in the early church and has yet to be accomplished. The logic of the passage suggests that the ministry of apostle (along with the rest and understood in the second category of which we have spoken) is still necessary in some form for the progress of the church.

The case from church history

The case may now be pursued historically. In different forms, the church has evidenced from its beginnings an instinct for some form of translocal, overseeing ministry. The precise origins of episcopacy are not easy to discern. It is evident, however, that the church of the post-apostolic period saw developing a threefold ministry in the form of bishop, presbyter and deacon. This marked a distinguishing of the roles of *episkopos* and *presbuteros*, whereas these terms described one role in the New Testament. As the church grew, those who were bishops of local congregations began to oversee daughter churches and assumed responsibility for areas and regions, until dioceses emerged and so the office of bishop was conceived of in broader terms.

In the growth of the church there is an inherent dynamic which makes for the multiplication of congregations without severing existing pastoral ties. Pastors of congregations tend then to assume wider spheres of influence. The same is to be observed in the growth of later denominations, which create patterns of translocal oversight appropriate to their situation even if they do not use the word 'bishop'. Methodists have circuits of churches under the oversight of a senior superintendent minister. The circuits are then overseen by the chairman of the district. In the early years of the growth of Methodism in the USA, the equivalent holder of this position was ordained a bishop and this still applies. The same position in the United Reformed Church is called a moderator. In the early twentieth century the English Baptist Union appointed area superintendents.

In the USA, several of the Mennonite groups which descended from the Anabaptists ordain bishops as the highest order of ministry within their ranks. This is particularly significant because of their commitment to the principle of the gathered church and its autonomy. It is an explicit attempt to combine an advisory, translocal bishoping role with the autonomy of the local congregation. They were not always successful in doing so and some bishops attempted to exceed the legitimate boundaries of their service, but it has also been made to work well. For Baptists, there is a particular part of their heritage which is worth retrieving at this point and it concerns the office of 'messenger', which was common particularly among General Baptists of the seventeenth and eighteenth centuries.

In 1958, John Nicholson, himself later to become an area superintendent, published an article on the subject of the office of messenger among British Baptists. His conclusion was that:

> The history...of the role of messenger amongst both General and Particular Baptists shows the value of some form of bishop (neither group was afraid of the term), whose prime duty would be evangelism, and whose other duties such as visitation, administration and ordination would be subsidiary to that.

He also quotes from previous Baptist historians to the effect that:

> ...ever attentive...to the precedent of Scripture, it was not long before [the Baptists] supposed that they had discovered in the primitive churches an office superior to an elder. They remarked that Barnabas, Luke, Timothy and Titus and several others were fellow labourers with the apostles in the preaching of the gospel and the planting and regulating of churches; and that in various passages they are called apostles, or in English, messengers of the churches (Adam Taylor).[8]

Similarly:

The first distinctive feature was the recognition of the duty of evangelisation, and telling off special men for itinerant work. Seeing that the early church commissioned men for special journeys, as with Judas, Silas, Barnabas, Tychicus, they formally commissioned men, and gave them the same title, messengers. At first there was a special commission for each journey; soon they selected men who had particular aptitude for evangelisation, told them off for it as their main work, and undertook to support them and their families. Thus the title messenger came to have a technical meaning, and since the cost of support was often more than a single church could sustain constantly, each messenger was linked with a group of churches. While evangelisation was the main purpose, there followed from it the duty of organising new communities, and counselling them in their early days. Men who had the double gift [presumably of evangelism and pastoring] were of use also in the older churches which maintained and commissioned them, and thus came to be invoked whenever internal troubles arose (W. T. Whitley).[9]

The fullest justification of the office was published first in 1671 with the title *A Defence of the Office of Apostles; and of the Continuance Thereof in the Church till the End*, written by Thomas Grantham. Grantham argued that there were no apostles in the sense of the original twelve, to whom was given 'an infallible revelation to lay an infallible foundation'. But in the following respects apostles still exist:

1. In respect of lawful power or authority to preach the gospel in all places, at all times, to all persons, as occasion and opportunity by God's providence shall be given them.
2. Unwearied diligence in teaching and strengthening both pastors and churches (chiefly those which are but newly settled in the faith) in all the council of God; and by labouring to perfect that which is lacking concerning the faith of any churches.
3. In being set for a defence of the gospel, or doctrine once delivered, against false apostles, or such as would introduce false doctrine; and also to strengthen the hands of particular pastors against usurpers, or such as despise the ministry of Christ.

Against the charge that such an office leads to that of an

Anglican bishop, Grantham qualified it, according to Nicholson:

> ...by pointing out that every church has the right to send forth such ministers, who remain members of that church subject to its discipline, and that their pre-eminence is only a degree of honour, not of power.

This line of thought is developed in the words of *An Orthodox Creed* in 1679, which specifically speaks of bishops who are:

> ...chosen thereunto by the common suffrage of the Church, and solemnly set apart by prayer and fasting, with imposition of hands by the bishops of the same function, ordinarily, and those bishops ordained have the government of those churches, that had suffrage in their election, and no other ordinarily; as also to preach the word or gospel to the world or unbelievers.

The office of messenger was by no means universally accepted among Baptists and, in time, declined along with the general decline of the cause in the seventeenth century. Yet the information we have gleaned is of great interest. It points to the priority of church planting and evangelism in the role of the messenger. Once this element was lost the office began to decline. It sees as secondary but necessary the ministry of advising existing churches, by supporting their pastors, particularly against those who despised the ministry they exercised, and by protecting from false teaching. Significantly, they could only function in the churches which recognised them and appointed them and had no authority elsewhere other than in generally preaching the gospel. They remained members of local churches, were accountable to them and were supported financially by the churches acting in association. Some were recognised as having a 'double gift', qualifying them as evangelists and pastoral advisers.

Of great interest is the fact that the word 'messenger' is a translation of 'apostle' and that the word 'bishop' was also used to describe this ministry. Baptist history gives evidence

of experimentation with apostolic/bishoping ministries. It also
indicates that there are deep-seated influences at work which
seek to find expression in these forms of ministry in the
church. To those influences our attention now turns.

The case from current practice

In seeking to construct a case for Baptist bishops, I now
adduce the theory and principles of church growth. In church
growth terms, there is a need to set apart tried and tested
ministers to oversee and develop the mission of the churches.
It is characteristic of the British scene that ministerial
development is not seen in apostolic, outward thrusting terms.
Rather, ministers are considered to have achieved some success when they have developed expository, teaching ministries. What is modelled to the rest of the church as a
consequence of this is a static ministry which sees the edifica-
tion of the saints as the highest value. It further confirms the
churches in their willingness to invest in ministries which
directly benefit them but not in those which will produce
results beyond their orbit. Yet, where we choose to invest our
best resources of people will determine the shape of the
future.

One way in which the process could be reversed would be
to develop a progression in ministry whereby the most effective and competent ministers were encouraged to move into
apostolic, missionary roles. This does not conflict with the
secondary function of caring for existing churches, since the
front line of mission is the place from which the development
of church life may best be seen in perspective. If the formation
of local churches has to do with their effectiveness in mission,
those who are most engaged in mission are in a position to
give the most pertinent advice. It does mean that ways would
need to be found to support such ministries financially and
practically, and that patterns of retraining and reorientation
might need to be developed to bring it to pass. The overall
effect would be to sharpen the focus of the church on those

things which are really necessary, a move from maintenance to mission.

Yet, the maintenance of the churches is not to be downgraded. There is little point in winning people if they are not going to be formed in Christ-like discipleship within a caring community. Furthermore, the quality of a church's life and its effectiveness in mission are intimately related. The life of the church is a primary tool in evangelistic work. A church can scarcely work for the creation of a more Christ-like world if it is not itself becoming more like him. This task belongs of course to the work of the pastor-teacher but there are many reasons why a church might need to draw upon the resources of the wider church.

For a start, pastors who become immersed in the needs of a local community are apt to lose the vision of the whole. To preserve a church from insularity and help it to keep a perspective on its life, it is helpful for it to have external reference points which will relate it to the life of the church more generally. Further, no pastor is omnicompetent. Churches which receive one person's ministry for a consistent period of time will be apt to reproduce the strengths and the weaknesses of that ministry. As all have weaknesses, it is helpful for a church to be exposed to other forms of ministry particularly from people who know the church well and are able to identify where it may be weak. There is a peculiar chemistry at work in these things. Sometimes a visiting preacher is able to say difficult things with greater freedom. Often, a word brought by an outsider will be heard with new ears and may serve to capitalise upon the regular teaching which has been given.

From time to time, every church encounters problems which it struggles to resolve. These may be to do with personalities, or with questions of direction, disagreement and, sometimes, of doctrine. When this happens it is invaluable if it is understood that there are sounding-boards whose advice may be sought and taken. As most such problems will be complex, it is essential that there are those who know the life of a church well. Sound advice usually proceeds from the knowledge of a situation and the personalities involved. To be able to submit a problem to the counsel of a knowledgeable and caring person who is outside the situation can bring resolution to an impasse and open up progress. Even where problems are few, the knowledge that such persons are there in the background can bring security to a fellowship.

A bishoping function can assist the health of a congregation and help it in all stages of its life. There is need of more than occasional contact with such persons. What is required is consistent involvement, enabling the building of trusting relationships.

A further area of great importance concerns the care of church leaders, especially of pastors. The pastoral care and development of the pastors is a neglected task among Baptist Christians, despite the excellent work of heavy-laden superintendents. This neglect has led to the underdevelopment of the gifts which have been available and to the loss of able people because of disillusionment, breakdown and exhaustion. No one can pretend that pastoring is not a stressful task; the light of faith does not always burn strong and some personal problems will not be avoided, however supportive others may be. There is much work to do in caring for the carers.

At the moment there is in place in the Baptist Union a support system in the form of its superintendents, which enables those who are conscious of need to seek help. Alternatively, in times of crisis, pastors may go in the direction of other people whom they have known from the past and whom they trust. Increasingly, the awareness grows that this is not itself enough, that forms of care offering regular support and review of spiritual and vocational progress are necessary and that the whole area of spiritual direction needs to be paid new attention.

It is striking that most caring professions now build team structures and support systems into their organisation. The objective is to help staff come to terms with their inner responses to the situations with which they are presented and the people with whom they deal, recognising the inner cost that is involved and the danger of leaving people without their own sources of support. An important spin-off is that such reflection adds to the insight with which the carer can return to the task. It improves the work that they do. For pastoral ministry such an approach is virtually unknown. It is difficult to quantify the long-term effect of this absence of support but it must take its toll and may contribute to withdrawal from ministry in some cases. The health of the churches is tied up with that of its leaders and more attention needs to be given to providing them with ongoing support from others who understand the pressures.

Another side to this coin is that people need to develop and if they do not, they grow stale. If one of the major resources of Baptist churches is its pastors, called by God and extensively trained at considerable expense, their ongoing development should be taken with the greatest seriousness. To their regular support needs to be added the facility for occasional review and possibilities for development. These various functions point to the fulfilling of bishoping roles on the part of some pastors.

Put together, the biblical, historical and practical considerations outlined here amount to a strong case for the bishoping function. Of the many further questions which are raised, we shall concern ourselves with three. How does what has been said relate to the existence of area superintendents? How may new patterns of bishoping/apostolic ministry emerge? What should such people be called?

Area superintendents

Early on in the twentieth century, Baptists in membership with the Baptist Union took a radical step and appointed ten ministers to serve in the newly created role of general superintendent. Their number has now risen to twelve and they have responsibility for the well-being of the churches in their appointed areas and especially for the ministers. They are available to give advice and general leadership and to facilitate the movement and settlement of ministers. Although a radical step at the time, the precedent of the office of messenger meant that their appointment was not a total departure from Baptist practice. In biblical terms, the justification of the office must appeal to the dimensions of ministry broader than the local church to which we have already drawn attention. It appears, however, that there are at least three differences (apart from the name) between the messengers and the current practice of superintendency.

First, the superintendents do not have church-planting and evangelism as their primary function, although it is one of the seven stated functions which they are to fulfil. The waning of this ingredient contributed to the decline of the office of messenger in earlier generations. Superintendents are not generally appointed for their evangelistic zeal, but for their overall pastoral ability and good sense. Essential though these qualities are in the fulfilment of the caring and advisory tasks, they inevitably orientate the role towards maintenance rather than mission. The fact that a superintendent has seven functions to fulfil tends to mean in practice that each one selects from them according to his own gifts and interests.

Secondly, the superintendents have responsibility for large geographical areas and for far more churches than they are able to serve in any other than an occasional capacity. Their time is well taken up with helping to settle new ministers, providing advice in extraordinary situations, administration and general preaching. By contrast, the messengers were involved with a far smaller number of churches and were consequently able to give more attention on an individual basis to existing churches and to devote time and effort to church-planting.

Thirdly, whereas the messengers were appointed by a single church or a cluster of churches acting together, superintendents are currently appointed as employees of the Baptist Union. The effect of this appointment must be that the loyalty of superintendents is with the institution that employs them and this will shape the agenda for their work. This is unlikely to make for radical and adventurous action. In recent years, associations have sought to cater for the wider needs of their churches by new forms of appointment including church-planters and evangelists, sometimes called association ministers or missioners. The possibilities of further experiment are there in the present system and are being widely taken up. Superintendents fulfil a vital function and are the objects of much affection and appreciation. But in the light of the immensity of the tasks, the question of the development of bishoping/apostolic ministries arises. What new patterns might emerge?

New patterns of ministry

New patterns might arise on the formal and informal levels and we shall begin with the formal. Any suggestions that I might make here are in part dependent upon a previous change for which I have argued, namely a decentralising shift of finance and influence from the centre towards the present associations and whatever new patterns of association might develop in a more organic and flexible Baptist Union. This would involve associations in appointing their own superintendents from below and would leave the door open even more widely than it is at present for them to experiment with new patterns. As some superintendents at the moment serve more than one association, a new freedom could lead to more such ministers serving fewer churches each. With this may be combined the existing trend to develop teams around superintendents to supplement their activity and fulfil functions which it is not possible for any one person to do.

The possible permutations of such teams are considerable and could involve part-time, full-time and consulting roles. Pastors might divide their time between one church and wider responsibilities. Others might act as consultants (for instance in church growth, counselling in specialist areas, spiritual direction, charismatic renewal, dealing with the demonically oppressed, theological education and training, music ministries) in full- or part-time capacities for one or several associations. It would be necessary that those appointed as senior members of such teams should have evangelism and mission as the heart of their concern, since only when this is the focus will the rest be in perspective.

The picture I am painting here of the proliferation of ministries is only possible where there is vision for growth and progress. Where these are to be found, the money that enables these things to happen will be forthcoming. There is a parallel here with what is now visible at the local level. Many more churches are able to employ multiple staff and in time this will be reflected in the association life of the churches.

What I have described here as part of what is formally possible is only part of the picture. At the informal level, there are other possibilities which it ought to be the task of the formal level to encourage. There are pastoral leaders who develop bishoping and apostolic abilities which cannot be expressed in their own churches and who need a sphere in which to exercise their gifts. These may be pastors who, while remaining in one church, become resource persons for other churches and other leaders. Those churches who have folk like this in leadership should learn how to make their own pastors available to others, recognising that the broadening experience thus gained will bring benefits back into the church.

Others may be retired pastors who draw upon their years of experience to impart wise counsel and good teaching where it is needed. Yet others may develop itinerant ministries with special emphases, while remaining accountable within a local church. Some may be in other employment and yet able to give themselves to wider service. The practical possibilities are very considerable and in some measure already exist. The need is to strengthen what is already there and to allow for new possibilities by acknowledging the need for that aspect of Christian ministry which we have been calling the bishoping/apostolic dimension.

New names

Our final question, then, concerns what names should be used to describe those who minister in these ways. At the informal level, it would seem appropriate simply to recognise that certain people fulfil functions which may be described in bishoping or apostolic terms. There is no real need to go beyond this and bestow titles. At the formal level, descriptive titles become more necessary, but to speak of the general superintendent sounds increasingly ponderous and awkward. The word 'apostle' is biblical but can hardly be used without explanation; the Baptist version, 'messenger', says little that would be meaningful to the modern ear. The word 'bishop' is perhaps the best alternative from the ones we have so far used, since it has pastoral and spiritual overtones and is hallowed by historical usage and custom.

It may be best of all, however, if the simple and modest custom prevailed of speaking of area or association ministers, who are to a group of churches what the local pastors are to their church, servants whose authority comes from the knowledge, love and call of Christ which has been recognised in them. Yet despite this modest title, we should not hesitate to speak of the apostolic or bishoping function they fulfil, since this is a reminder both to them and those whom they serve of the high calling of God in Christ.

The intent of this chapter has been to argue that ministry in the church is full of variety and opportunity. The days of the traditional one-man-one-church approach to pastoral care are fast disappearing. Not only do we now see that both men and women are called to pastoral leadership in churches in which all members are called to be ministers, but also that there are varieties of ministries designed to be deployed in recognised roles within and beyond the local congregation. Superintendents are more than a useful idea. They are a way of recognising the breadth of the ministry which Christ has set in the church for its well-being. Further experimentation in ministry is needed for the good of the church and as a way of providing broader opportunities for those who are called to full-time availability to the church to fulfil their callings, maintain their freshness and increase their capacities.

There is no doubt that at present there is a mood for experiment which may well permit the wider dimensions of the apostolic ministry to come to expression. Within this there is the need for men and women of extraordinary spiritual stature to emerge, with the shepherding skills to care for the wider flock and the prophetic insight to see clearly where God is leading his people. A drawback of the congregational approach to church life is that we hold such people back by not allowing them sufficient scope for leadership or by failing to encourage them along the way. Yet such leadership is needed. It is important to be able to look to leaders who are distinguished, not in their ability to administer a large organisation effectively (although this is a wonderful gift), but in their closeness to Christ and resemblance to him.

The recognition that the apostolic ministry—that is, the ministry in the church of which the New Testament speaks—is broader than the local and that we all need to benefit from it may be the soil out of which the next generation will grow.

8

Called to Nonconform

Baptists are nonconformists. Technically, this term describes the position of those who do not conform to the doctrine and practices of the established church. The word was first used of those who left the Church of England rather than submit to the Act of Uniformity in 1662, which sought, as its title suggests, to impose religious conformity by force of law. Such folk were originally called dissenters, but this name gave way eventually to nonconformists. Yet the technical word bears testimony to something deeper and it is with this that we are chiefly concerned.

From the beginning, Baptist believers have been at odds with the established order. They have acknowledged a higher duty than that to the king or state, namely the duty to obey God's will as made known in Christ. For their contemporaries, the distinction was hard to understand. For centuries, the powers of the state and of religion had worked together. In England, the king was believed by many to govern by divine right. Obedience to the king was obedience to God, a religious duty.

The Baptists called this into question because they saw clearly that at some points the power of the king was in conflict with their conscientious duty to God. The form of church life which they believed to be according to God's will was the object of persecution and opposition on the part of the civil authorities. This put the king on the side of the Antichrist. In recognising that Caesar might demand something that was contrary to Christ, they grasped an important spiritual principle of the 'crown rights of the redeemer', that is, the supremacy of the will of Christ for the church, come what may. Coincidentally, they were undermining the totalitarian powers of the state. It is no surprise that they were regarded as politically subversive—this is precisely what they were, although perhaps even they failed to recognise to what extent.

In this chapter we are concerned to investigate what it means to be a nonconformist now. To do this we shall need to discuss some of the ways in which Baptist Christians have expressed their nonconformity in the past and the relevance of this agenda for today. Our final conclusion will be that much of the agenda remains and needs to be re-appropriated, but that as it has been hitherto conceived, it is restricted in scope. A new look at nonconformity from a biblical perspective must be taken if we are to be truly faithful to the will of God and the essential Baptist vision of the church.

From the beginning, Baptist believers have been in conflict with the majority opinion concerning the nature of the church. They have opposed the idea of Christendom, the idea that the church and the political state are able to coalesce into one religio-political reality. This concept of the partnership of religion and politics is an ancient one. Most pre-Christian societies were sacral. Leonard Verduin describes a sacral society thus:

> A sacral society has a single religiosity at its heart, an ultimate loyalty of soul, which, it is assumed, is common to each member of that society. In a sacral society one's religion is a matter of course, determined by one's inclusion in the societal unit...In a sacral society there is unanimity on the religious plane, the plane on which man's deepest loyalties lie.[10]

Religion has been commonly understood as the glue which holds a society together. Nonconformity to the established religion cannot be tolerated, since it is a threat to the well-being of the tribe or nation. It is for this reason that the early Christians were persecuted. They dissented from the established religion of the Roman Empire. Rome had worked out an ingenious system of religious syncretism. Many gods were tolerated as long as their devotees did not make exclusive claims. When new tribes were conquered, their gods were co-opted into the existing Pantheon and a state of peaceful co-existence reigned. The cement which held the Empire together was devotion to the Emperor as to a god and lord. All religions were tolerated which were prepared to accommodate to this state of affairs.

There was one exception, the Jews, who were regarded as so unreasonable that they were allowed for most of the time to carry on in their own way. The Jews would not acknowledge any god but the Lord. When Rome ignored their sensitivities rebellion would follow, so as long as Judaism was confined to a particular ethnic group the Jews were tolerated as an oddity.

When Christianity burst upon the scene, such an uneasy compromise became impossible. Like the Judaism from which it sprang, it made exclusive claims. The true God was alone to be worshipped and Jesus Christ, not Caesar, was Lord. Unlike Judaism, it was aggressively evangelistic, had an uncanny ability to spread and was winning converts rapidly. This posed a threat to the cohesion of the Empire, since Jesus Christ was not a candidate for co-option. The Christians were nonconformists and were politically dangerous as such. For their part, the Christians regarded the alliance of the state with a blasphemous religious system as an expression of the power of Antichrist which had its origin in hell.

It is in the context of this irreversible clash between two different modes of thought that the sporadic persecutions of the early church are to be understood. And yet, the blood of the martyrs proved to be the seed of the church. The more the persecution, the swifter the growth. This continued until a truly brilliant idea was conceived. Since Christianity was undefeatable, why not make a total about turn and make it the 'single religiosity' at the heart of the Roman Empire? This process was accomplished in the fourth century, beginning with the Edict of Milan in 313 AD, which declared toleration for the church. Gradually, the Christianisation of the Empire was accomplished.

Many Christians believed that the millennium had arrived. It felt like the triumph of the sons of light over the sons of darkness. The Old Testament appeared to offer a model of how the nations could fuse the power of the state with true religion. The time of suffering was past and the Lord was vindicating his people. But in retrospect it is clear, at least to some, that the legalising of the Christian religion in this particular fashion was the greatest disaster to have befallen the church in all its history. The Empire may in part have been Christianised, but at the cost of paganising the church, importing into the faith a foreign and destructive spirit and subjecting it to the far from Christian concerns of the state.

Once more, religion was being used in the service of political power and social cohesion, but in a way which transformed the religion of the cross into something quite different. The persecuted minority became the persecuting majority. The little flock became the established authority. Freely chosen discipleship became self-seeking nominal allegiance. In time, the badge of this distortion of the church of the apostles was infant baptism, by which the 'single religiosity' was enforced and the power of the church extended. This religio-political hybrid called Christendom has endured and has been the enemy of true religion and of nonconformity ever since.

The genius of the Anabaptists was that they saw this state of affairs for what it was. They believed that in the fourth century the church had fallen as surely as had Adam at the dawn of history. It was now their responsibility to work for the restitution of the true church. The rejection of infant baptism, the gathering of true believers and the non-sacramental breaking of bread were the first steps in this direction. But more was demanded of the disciple. Because the state was hopelessly compromised, the disciple must not compromise with it. The majority of Anabaptists developed an antipathy to the state, born of the fierce persecutions and rough justice they suffered at its hands. Behind this was the ideology of the sacral state which they believed to be hostile to the faith. The Anabaptists believed that, though the powers that be were instituted by God within their own sphere, their fallen condition meant that Christians were unable to fall in with their wrongful exercise of power. This nonconformity was expressed in three symbolic ways.

First, Anabaptists in general (with the exception of the Münster rebellion in 1535) refused as a matter of principle to take up the sword either for or against the political power. In the words of Conrad Grebel, 'Neither do they use worldly sword or war, since all killing has ceased with them.'[11] In 1755, the principle of non-violence was summarised by a group of Mennonite ministers in Pennsylvania as follows:

> It is our fixed principle rather than take up arms to defend our king, our country or ourselves, to suffer all that is dear to us to be rent from us, even life itself, and this we think not out of contempt to authority, but that herein we act agreeable to what we think is the mind and will of the Lord Jesus.

This stance must be seen against the background of the use of the sword to enforce religious beliefs and conformity. Once the false system and demands of the state have been seen through, it becomes nonsensical to kill in its service as well as being inconsistent with the teaching of Christ.

Secondly, Anabaptists as a rule refused to serve as magistrates. The state was allied with a religious system which they regarded as unholy, and it was the responsibility of the magistrate to enforce the state's religious demands. This would have produced an impossible clash of loyalties for those who saw themselves as seeking to restore the true church. They could not serve the interests of the false church. They might even end up persecuting their fellow believers.

This was allied to a third concern. Anabaptists generally refused to swear or take oaths in a court of law, believing this to be contrary to the teaching of Jesus in Matthew 5:33–37. Inevitably this alienated them from the civil processes which depended upon the administration of the oath. Anabaptists were required by their convictions to practise civil disobedience and were heavily persecuted as obstinate nonconformists as a consequence. How much of their nonconforming legacy is valid for our age remains to be seen.

Our attention now turns to the English Baptists who emerged in the seventeenth century in two denominations, the General Baptists, stemming from the church founded in Amsterdam in 1609 by John Smyth and Thomas Helwys, and the Particular Baptists, emerging from the separatist wing of the Puritan movement in the 1630s. In the early stages, the General Baptists showed traces of Anabaptist influence, but generally the nonconformity of the English groups took a different form. While arguing for religious liberty and the reform of the state church, they were neither pacifists, nor opposed to the magistracy nor generally persuaded concerning refusal of the oath.

Indeed, as the century wore on, Baptists were prepared, along with other Independents, to take up arms against the government of king and church and to fight for religious liberty with the sword in what they saw to be a holy war. Baptists were prominent in the parliamentary army and are said to have comprised its backbone. The growth of Baptist churches in the period 1640–60 owes a great deal to the movement of Baptist soldiers and their evangelistic zeal wherever they were stationed. Many of the most radical of Cromwell's troops were Baptist Christians, and he had a hard time keeping some of them in line.

This is a different approach to nonconformity from that of the continental Anabaptists, and it differs principally in its attitude to the state. Far from distancing themselves from the levers of power, Baptists were prepared to fight for them, both physically and politically, in order to capture them for the service of religious liberty. It is unquestionable that to an extent they succeeded. The British parliamentary system has been indelibly marked by the so-called Great Rebellion, and as a consequence of it, though with a struggle, constitutional monarchy and parliamentary democracy have emerged. But those who fought and gained the ascendancy became involved themselves in the inevitable ambiguities of worldly power.

The progress of Cromwell (himself an Independent or Congregationalist rather than a Baptist, although sympathetic to them) from champion of the people to virtual dictator, is symbolic of this. Neither did he achieve true religious liberty since, having removed one form of coercion he proceeded to institute another in the interests of true religion as conceived by him. John Milton could complain that under this regime 'new presbyter is but old priest writ large'. The enduring message of Cromwell for us is that he knew what he opposed in the church and society of his day and believed it to be pleasing to God that society should be made more conformable to God's will; but as to what a new society should look like and how it might be achieved, he was not so sure, and hardly surprisingly since it had rarely been attempted before in quite this way.

In retrospect, we can see that in attempting to impose the rule of the saints upon the ungodly, Cromwell came near to repeating the worst features of the old regime and may even have exceeded them. While we cannot say that he was supported all along the way by Baptists, he was none the less illustrating the fact that early nonconformity had not yet discovered how to relate to the state without betraying its own principles.

We have observed how Anabaptists adopted a nonconformity which led them to disengage from the power structures of their society. Many English Baptists practised a nonconformity which led them in an opposite direction—to challenge the power structures, seeking to change them by force. In the nineteenth century, developments took place which may provide a further observable stance, the growth of the so-called nonconformist conscience which developed as nonconformists realised that democratic forms of political action had the potential to change society for good. In the course of the nineteenth century, nonconformists gained greater access to Parliament, by virtue of the widening franchise and their own burgeoning numbers and growing economic power. Many of the new industrialists were nonconformist by conviction. Progressively, the Liberal Party, which was their natural home, in contrast to the landed and aristocratic interests of the Tories, became the vehicle of their political self-expression. In the 1890s the nonconformist conscience was identified. David Bebbington has chronicled its rise and describes its features as follows:

> Those features were three: a conviction that there is no strict boundary between religion and politics; an insistence that politicians should be men of the highest character; and a belief that the state should promote the moral welfare of its citizens. All were new in the late Victorian period. Previously Nonconformists had assumed a contrast between Christian work and worldly activity, with politics decidedly on the wrong side of the divide, legitimate but risky. They had, of course, hoped that politicians would be men of personal integrity, but had not supposed that this could be treated as a qualification for the office. And they had argued that because the state was likely to harm its citizens by decreasing their self-reliance, it should confine itself to a narrow sphere of interference in their lives. All these attitudes were characteristic of people who felt politics to be an alien world. That was beginning to change.[12]

The belief that public service was a responsibility was well established and already carried through by many at a local level. This was now to be supplemented by the view that politics could be a high calling and that everything is religious which is not irreligious. Through democratic means, the law could be captured for the service of the people's moral well-being. Indeed, the gospel alone could make them truly moral, but the law could play an educational as well as a coercive role in guiding public opinion away from what was immoral. This, allied to voluntary action, could produce a better society.

There is little doubt that this new awareness on the part of nonconformists had an effect in bringing positive change. In addition to the traditional hostility to the establishment of the Church of England by law (which they never succeeded in changing, although many of the attendant abuses were reformed), nonconformists took to the lists over the moral issues of their day as they understood them. Yet here the weakness of the nonconformist conscience was revealed. By employing in social issues a crusading technique which tapped into evangelical hostility to sin and treated social wrongs as evils to be defeated, they were able to mobilise mass support on selective issues. But as such, their aims were negative. They knew what they were against, but could not bring proposals of anything new.

Further, because they saw themselves as being against sin, they became intransigent, unable to compromise and often extreme or exaggerated in their rhetoric. 'Indignation meetings' were a tool of their political influence. The shortcomings of this approach to politics need to be pondered today, when evangelical churches are undergoing a politicisation akin to the growth of the nonconformist conscience. Now, as then, the tendency is to launch crusades around single issues which can be identified as sin. When this is the case it is inevitable that there will be an emotional response from the believing population, that there will be a tendency to use heightened language and rhetoric, and these factors make it difficult to compromise and lead to the alienation of others involved in the political process.

In the absence of any coherent political philosophy apart from these issues to serve as a guide for action, there is a tendency for opinion to be led by whatever is being promoted or exposed in the press at a given time. The agenda is not according to a balanced political philosophy but is set by forces external to the church. Christians agree on what they are against but have difficulty deciding what they are for. In consequence, the possibility of taking action in favour of positive and constructive, as opposed to preventative, political change seems to elude them. They are among the political reactors rather than the creative actors.

What we have been doing is to review in a selective fashion some of the nonconforming attitudes that have been expressed among Baptists of previous generations. Plainly, their story has often intertwined with that of other like-minded believers. What has been revealed is a conviction that the kind of church-state society which first persecutes dissenters and then discriminates against them when they cannot be eradicated is unChristian. United in this, they have been divided in believing what should be done and by what means. The Anabaptists were, by and large, so far alienated from the system that they could only contemplate a respectful withdrawal. It is easy to characterise this stance as quietism and separatism, but it should not so easily be rejected.

They grasped that the state ultimately is about power and coercion and, while they believed it to be instituted of God in its own worldly sphere for the restraint of sin, they believed there had to be limits to the involvement in state affairs of those who were in 'the perfection of Christ' and who were called to live according to a new kingdom. Those who walked in the Messiah's way of suffering and self-giving love could hardly participate in the unloving and coercive power politics of the state, especially when to do so meant compromise with the false form of religion intimately involved with it. The best thing was to follow Christ humbly and suffer for him if need be. And they did.

The danger they intuitively perceived, of being forced to play according to the world's rules, is amply illustrated by the struggle of English Baptists in the Civil War and by the nonconformist conscience. In taking up arms in the name of religious liberty, the Baptist warriors distinguished themselves in battle but may have ended up committing the same bloody sins as the sacral state, only doing so in zeal for the Lord and his righteousness. The remarkable story of Oliver Cromwell, himself a devout and in many ways admirable Puritan believer, illustrates the dictum that power corrupts. It was not that he became corrupt personally, but that the demands of power required unChrist-like methods. It is one thing to remove a system and another to replace it with a better.

The thought of a totalitarian system operated by those who are quite convinced of their own righteousness and the unrighteousness of their enemies is strangely chilling. The democratic and persuading approach of the nonconformist conscience is a better model, but illustrates a new set of dangers. Chief among these must be the limitations of the crusading approach, the tendency to see only certain issues and to neglect others and the absence of a progressive political philosophy. The nonconformist is thus reduced to reacting to an agenda someone else has set, while creative political progress is left to others. There must certainly be a reform of abuses but this is not enough on its own for responsible political action.

Moreover, the temptation always remains to seek for political power to advance the interests of a section of society rather than the whole, or possibly to impose upon society as a whole what is perceived to be good for it by one section which has superior knowledge. In asserting the need for a nonconformity for today, three issues need to be faced. The first concerns the relation between Christian faith and politics, the second the development of a true understanding of the state and of political action and the third, the role of the church.

Concerning the first, we do not intend to say a great deal, other than to affirm agreement with that feature of the nonconformist conscience which understood there to be no strict boundary between religion and politics. Because all things owe their being to God, politics must be a legitimate sphere of Christian concern and it is a duty to seek to take every thought captive to make it obedient to Christ. Quietism, the belief that the church and state must each go their own way, is itself a type of conformity to the status quo and therefore a political position. Christian concern for the state must always be active. Yet it will not always take the same form. If the strategy determined by the kingdom of God is that we must work for the reconciliation of all things, the tactics vary according to the witness required in particular situations.

This will sometimes mean that Christians who share the convictions outlined in this book will not feel able conscientiously to participate in the political process as such. Where a totalitarian regime requires what conscience cannot give, the witness is best exercised against the political process rather than within it. This was the position of the early Anabaptists and may need to be repeated in fascist or communist dictatorships. However, where the political process is not tied to a sacral or totalitarian concept of the state, the witness may be exercised from within the system with good conscience. Whatever the tactical decision, the concern must be to seek the welfare of the place where we find ourselves and this responsibility cannot be renounced. In our own country, with such democratic freedoms as have been won over the years, there is every reason for a witness from within.

The second issue concerns the nature of the state and of political action, and is complex. There are at least three ways of approaching the state and there is considerable confusion among Baptists about where their commitment lies. We have already noted that the Anabaptist and Baptist movements arose as protests against the concept of the sacral state, whereby primitive Christianity had been hijacked by political necessity and pressed into service. The result was a distortion of the faith against which renewal movements arose continually to protest, seeking to recapture the true devotion of the early church. The monastic movement should be seen in this light.

We live now in a much changed world, however. The state has been secularised and in our country only the vestiges of established religion remain, in the form of the Churches of England and of Scotland. Yet the vestiges are considerable.

The Queen is regarded as head of the Church of England and was herself anointed in office by the archbishops. Senior bishops sit in the House of Lords, the Prime Minister has power of appointment and Parliament retains some control over internal ecclesiastical legislation. The strange thing is that, while growing numbers in the established churches have come to see that this is in principle wrong because it conflicts with biblical faith, and others have come to see that it is practically nonsensical, Baptists have increasingly accorded it tacit approval. Disestablishment, for which Baptists have argued for centuries, is now regarded by some Baptists as yet another move in the direction of a totally secular state. The official sanction of Anglican religion is regarded as a bulwark against the growth of secularism.

I shall argue shortly that this is wrong-headed, but simply point out here that for Baptists to oppose disestablishment is a betrayal of the tradition we represent. No consistent Baptist can approve of the sacral state or anything that looks like it.

Having argued this, the next point is not so clear-cut. As I perceive it, there has been a division in Baptist opinion about the state from the beginning. I wish to distinguish between Puritan and Dissenting Baptists and these represent the second and third options on this issue.

Puritan Baptists I see as strongly influenced by Calvinist Presbyterianism in the seventeenth century which, while opposed to the form of religion espoused in the Church of England, nevertheless believed in the right and responsibility of the state to establish true religion and to promote reform. This is consistent with the position taken by the mainstream Reformers in Europe. The coercive role of the state in matters of religion is not rejected in principle, but in its particular expression. The Catholic Church was false religion and since the state was subject to God and bound to do his will, it must throw its weight on the side of the true faith, conceived of as Presbyterianism.

In the early stages of the Civil War, the parliamentary forces were a coalition of Presbyterians, Independents and

Baptists and were therefore divided between the Puritan and Dissenting options. Later, the differences were to emerge in no uncertain terms. Once it gained the upper hand, the Presbyterian-dominated Parliament sought to enforce its own brand of religious conformity. Even under the Commonwealth (Cromwell being instinctively sympathetic to Independents and Baptists) religious liberty was extended to cover a greater range of orthodox Christian opinion, but those regarded as unorthodox, particularly Catholics and Unitarians, or as blasphemers, were discriminated against and suppressed.

The point I am drawing from this is that Puritan Baptists past and present may be opposed to the establishment of one denomination by law but still believe that the state has a right and a responsibility to support the Christian religion in a Christian country and to enforce its standards.

It is for this reason that some Baptists have expressly disavowed disestablishment and the majority of others have lost interest in it. They see the issue as being now no longer between different denominations striving for recognition but of the faith surviving in the face of the forces of unbelief or, increasingly, in the face of militant alien beliefs, especially Islam. Vestiges of a one time Christian consensus, such as worship and Christian religious instruction in school, prayers in Parliament at the beginning of the day's business and the religious overtones of the monarchy are seen as bulwarks against unbelief which it is worth fighting to retain. This way of thinking is reflexive to many Baptist believers today. Yet I believe it to be wrong, since it capitulates to a view of the sacral state which, even in its moderated Puritan form, departs from New Testament faith.

What, then, of the third approach, which I have spoken of as the Dissenting Baptist position? I see this as the view which is closest to the New Testament, most consistent with Baptist principles and the most realistic in the modern world. This is the understanding that it is the duty of the state to renounce any form of coercion or of discrimination in matters of religion. This position opposes the sacral view by seeing the state in secular terms. It goes beyond the Puritan view in believing that it is not the place of the state to favour any religious position but to ensure and enhance the religious liberty of all its subjects. The state must deal even-handedly with those of any faith or of none.

The foundation of this view is that it is morally wrong to demand religious liberty and freedom from discrimination for oneself and deny them to others. Moreover, if it is believed that true religion cannot be coerced or compelled but must spring from a freely chosen faith, then the cause of true religion cannot be advanced by worldly power. This is not to say that the state cannot affect the progress of true religion, but that it does so by ensuring the freedom of its people and thereby providing the conditions which enable the preaching of the gospel to be carried on. It is the gospel that has power to persuade. Civil religion, that is, religious practices and ceremonies which are used in the service of the state, are deceptive for the same reason as is infant baptism. They encourage people to believe that it is possible to engage in Christian faith or worship without the heart-changing experience of regeneration.

The logic of this position carries us further, since it sees little or no spiritual value in the vestiges of the sacral state to which people are attached. 'Worship' in schools may have a cultural value in inducting children into hymn-singing and set prayers, but it is not worship in spirit and truth, except in the case of those who would willingly worship in their families and churches anyway. Spiritually, it runs the risk of hypocrisy and of hardening hearts by its unreality. A government which enforces it needs to be questioned hard, since its concern is more likely to be the production of a certain type of citizen than of believers born from above. Religious education certainly has its place in schools, but as education concerning a hugely important aspect of life, not instruction in an agreed creed. The ceremonial use of religion in state functions may be ceremonially satisfying but is not true spirituality. It substitutes priestcraft and tribal religion for discipleship.

A glaring example of this was the service of thanksgiving for victory in the Falklands War, where the political pressure was towards glorying in national pride and strength. This is not the faith of the cross but its opposite. The use of the Christian religion in this way is an attempt to co-opt it into being the domestic servant of the political power. The true church is not the guardian of the national spirit and heritage but the prophetic community of God's people in the midst of the nation. An established church has little hope of fulfilling this prophetic function since it is established to sanctify the status quo, not to criticise it.

The logic of the Dissenting position leads us to the secularisation of the state and the refusal to use its power to endorse any one religious confession so that the liberty of all may be enhanced. It affirms that the will of God is not best served by causing the state, through force or legislation, to serve one particular religious group but by causing it to provide the conditions in which ideas may be freely exchanged and allegiances changed. This does not mean that we give up the attempt to Christianise the state but that this open and tolerant kind of society is precisely the form that a Christianised society takes. This reflects the nature of the God revealed in Christ, who did not come to coerce but to draw people to himself by the power of his sacrificial love. It is a pluralist concept of the state because it refuses to legislate for conscience and is deliberately tolerant of diversity of opinion.

For those who believe in the persuasive power of the gospel, the idea of a pluralist society holds no terrors. It is worth noting that the Dissenting approach to religion is what lies at the basis of the American constitution and that the USA is the nation which has been organised most consistently along the lines of religious liberty. It is further worth noting that it contains possibly the highest proportion of believers of any nation on earth. Close examination of the American evangelical scene, particularly of the Baptist scene, might indicate that the distinction between Puritans and Dissenters accounts for different attitudes to the state in their ranks. There are those who would argue for a more bullish attempt to gain control of the apparatus of the state in order to back righteousness with power, to impose their version of morality upon the unwilling. Others affirm the role of the state not in enforcing the attitudes of some but in impartially creating the right conditions which will be for the good of all.

The same tendencies are discernible in the renewed political consciousness of believers in our own country and the attitudes distinguished above may help us. It is crucial that as evangelical Christians, Baptists among them, engage legitimately in the attempt to make the state serve the moral welfare of the people, they should be seen to be acting for the good of all, not just for the advancement of a sectional point of view, and certainly not in order to retain the vestige of some supposed sacral state. The Dissenting approach enables us to do this.

So we come to reflect upon the role and nature of the church in the light of what has been said and particularly that way of being the church embraced by Baptist Christians. The argument extended here is that Baptists must rediscover their own nonconforming heritage, including some of the issues which have concerned them in times past, and should develop their thinking further about the call to nonconform. From several quarters, the pressure is on no longer to think of ourselves as nonconformists.

One pressure is internal. Baptists have begun to adopt a conservative stance consistent with their own growth into respectability, their progress in social status and their involvement in the financial institutions of society. We no longer feel ourselves to be in the vanguard of social change but are fearful of it, characterising its proponents as subversive. We have a stake in the way things are.

External pressures also lead to the moderating of nonconformity. The ecumenical movement tends towards the suppression of old hostilities and makes for an accommodation to other models of being the church. The need to speak on equal terms with institutional church bodies, and to be accepted in their league, creates the pressure to be like them and to adopt their assumptions about themselves and others. From another source comes a similar pressure. The powerful pressure of interdenominational evangelical projects squeezes out what may be regarded by others as secondary issues but which are part of our primary witness. Such pressure would incline us to believe that personal conversion is the sum total of the gospel and that issues of the nature of the church take second place and may properly be suppressed for the sake of co-operation.

But the nature of the church as a believing community of disciples is intrinsic to the gospel, not secondary. It is for the sake of loyalty to the gospel and not to theological niceties that the nature of the new community is to be stressed and aberrant forms of the church rejected. This is not to denigrate co-operation, which is greatly to be encouraged, but to say that certain issues should be openly and continually debated and not treated as unimportant. Further, if this community is in the midst of the nations as a witnessing, prophetic people and is the agent of the kingdom of God, it is for the sake of the nations that it expresses true conformity to Christ in its form and existence. Issues that concern the way of being the church are by no means secondary and we should not allow them to be relegated. We need to discover the agenda from the past.

I would suggest that the core of this is opposition to the idea of a state church and the commitment to political reform in this area. The disestablishment of the Church of England, and the equivalent in Scotland, is necessary for the sake of the church, that it may be truly the fellowship of those who believe and may contradict the illusion that salvation is through birth rather than new birth. The radical reform of these church systems must surely follow. It is also necessary for the sake of the state, which is called to be the servant of God and of humanity in promoting the religious liberty of all its citizens impartially. From this must follow further reforms, including the repeal of all legislation which gives a privileged position to Anglican or Christian religion (the blasphemy laws being an example) and the introduction or extension of laws which will protect all and any people from religious hatred and prevent the infringement of their liberties.

The refusal of Anabaptists to swear oaths could be reconsidered as a point of witness. Swearing oaths on the Bible should be considered by Christians to be wrong, in the light of the teaching of Jesus in Matthew 5:33–37. It implies that there are levels of honesty, whereas Jesus taught that his disciples are always honest. Worse than this, it is a piece of hypocritical and magical mumbo-jumbo in a society which uses it as a legal device divorced from any possible spiritual meaning. We should work for its replacement at all levels of the system by a non-religious and equally effective affirmation. By refusing to swear on oath, Baptists could bear their testimony to a way of life based on the teaching of Jesus.

We should express our opposition to expressions of civil religion which have the form of religion but deny its power and use Christian traditions as a way of adding to the ceremony of the present. There should be no difficulty in finding appropriate ceremonial forms to enhance public life, without the need to co-opt the church for these tasks. By arguing from a Dissenting position for religious liberty and the state's impartiality, Christians could demonstrate in a pluralist society that they are not concerned to defend the last bastions of some religious empire but to treat their fellow citizens, of all faiths and of none, with respect and consideration. This would do more good for the cause of true religion than attempts to maintain a supposedly Christian culture.

These possible actions belong to the tradition from which we have come and are worth retrieving because they are valid. They are, however, restricted and are in danger of being negative. They are directed as a protest against the system in which our forebears found themselves. We need to go further and to return to a New Testament nonconformity such as is spoken of in Romans 12 and envisaged in many other places. Conformity to Jesus Christ leads to nonconformity to the world. The church has consistently reflected a captivity to the culture of the society in which it is set. We tend to assume society's values and fall into line with them. We reinforce these values by a selective and a slanted reading of the Bible in their favour.

The path to liberation from this cultural captivity lies along the lines perceived by the Anabaptists, and involves a refocusing upon Jesus Christ, who is the key to our understanding and behaviour and the centre of God's revelation of himself in Scripture as a whole. Working from this centre, much thinking has to be done about how believers live in today's society and engage with it socially and politically. The positive political philosophy which Baptist Christians need, to make them actors rather than reactors in the political realm, can be found by a renewed reflection on the meaning of Christ for the complexities of our world.

It is astonishing how few Christians work consistently from this centre. Jesus taught us to live in a way which is in keeping with the welfare of people and of the planet. He was manifested in our midst as the One through whom all things were made, who is the life and the light of humanity and who taught the things that make for peace—personal, social and political (Lk 19:42). True nonconformity is about hearing and following him against the tide of all that would flow against him. This is the kind of nonconformity that we should enter into: radical, Jesus-centred living, assisted by the community of God's people committed to the same pilgrimage.

Jesus told his disciples that they were the salt of the earth. Often enough this has been understood in negative terms. We are the disinfectant that stops the rot and keeps things from getting any worse. We certainly do not imagine that they will get much better. But another understanding is that salt is a fertiliser which causes that which is good to grow. Jesus himself had this influence wherever he was found. He caused the potential for good in people to come to expression and fellowshipped with tax-collectors and sinners to this end. The nonconformity to which we are called has its negative side, since what is wrong and false does need to be opposed. Yet the Christian witness centred on Christ has also the power to bring out that which makes for a better world and works towards the reconciliation of all things in the fullness of time. Baptists need to enter into this dimension of Christ-focused living to take them beyond their past into a better future of positive nonconformity.

9

Anabaptism as a Source of Renewal

I have made frequent reference in this book to the Anabaptists. To many, these people will be a mystery and therefore some attempt to introduce them is necessary. I am keen not to repeat what I have written on this subject in *The Radical Kingdom*, although I gave at that time only the shortest of sketches and one which took a particular point of view. I confess that I am not a disinterested historian (if there ever is such a person) who is merely interested in facts. The value of reading history is that it sheds light upon the present and gives signposts for the future. We are able to discern in it positive examples that we do well to follow and warnings of what it would be wise to avoid. Anabaptist history contains both, and reflection upon it can inspire and guide us as we work towards the renewal and reform of the church in our day. It can serve as a source for the work of renewal in which we are engaged now. I hope in this chapter to show some of the ways in which this may be true.

I need to come clean, however, and say that my enthusiasm for Anabaptists is not shared by everyone and it is possible to argue both ways about them. The story of Anabaptism is so varied and diverse that it is possible by a process of selection to praise it as a momentous leap forward or dismiss it as a fanatical delusion. As with many renewal movements before and after, the game of interpretation can be played according to different rules. We see exactly the same processes at work in, for instance, responses to present-day movements for renewal and restoration. Both can be criticised and enough negative evidence is around to construct a case against them.

Yet there is that at the core of each which cannot easily be rejected and which is, in my judgement, of God. We must penetrate through to that which is of God, and be true to it, while being wise enough to discern the false, the bad and the not so good. Conversely, we should recognise that none of us is strictly unbiased and that there are things which all of us are promoting, protecting or avoiding for reasons best known to ourselves. As a consequence, we argue against things because for personal reasons we may not like what we are hearing. Anabaptism has a way of evoking all these responses.

I freely confess that for myself the emergence of Anabaptism in the sixteenth century has a romantic power which I cannot fully explain. It seems to me that there are seasons in history where something hugely important breaks into our world and unleashes a creative force. It might be argued that this is true in all spheres of human endeavour, in scientific discovery or artistic innovation for instance, and that there is an element of inspiration involved in this which the believer would refer to God. Often, such luminous moments are the product of humanly understandable forces coming together and producing an opening in history which leaves things permanently different. Yet beyond this there is a further dimension which it is not easy to explain, a spiritual quality or constraint that seems to come from beyond. I see Anabaptism in this light, as a movement in which God gave illumination into his truth for the good of his church and of humankind as a whole.

In essence, Anabaptism is the emergence in the 1520s, the time of the Reformation, of varied groups of believers who believed in the gathered church, believers' baptism and religious liberty. Historically, the first group to be formed was in

Zürich and came into being on January 21st, 1525 when the first believers' baptisms of the modern age were performed. It is tempting to take this group as the norm and see all others in relation to it. The picture is not so simple. The left wing of the Reformation was far more chaotic than that. Some historians claim to have found some twenty discernible groups who may be termed Anabaptist, although only six of these proved to be of enduring importance.

The outstanding historian of the Radical Reformation (to employ yet another description), George H. Williams, argues that there were seven regional groupings and three 'morphological types' in Anabaptism. These types were, first, evangelical Anabaptists, comprising movements associated with the names of Conrad Grebel, Menno Simons, Jacob Hutter and Pilgram Marpeck. These he sees as advocating a 'suffering servant' form of discipleship and they are to be distinguished from the second type, Maccabean Münsterites, whom he describes as 'militant heralds'. This is the group that staged the violent revolution at Münster in 1535 and tarred the name of Anabaptism with this brush for centuries. These in turn are to be distinguished from a third grouping, spiritualising Anabaptists, whom he calls 'watchful brooders'. This category contains a host of groups with unorthodox tendencies and/or an emphasis on immediate inspiration.

From this categorisation it becomes immediately plain that, in their own day and subsequently, although these groups were lumped together, there were clear differences between them of which they were themselves conscious and which were the subject of debate. It must be added that in sociological terms there was some movement between the groups, as may be expected of an unstable movement at a time of ferment.

Williams goes on to make the point that by the end of the Reformation period, all but the first of these categories had disappeared or been converted into something else. It is for this reason that it is justifiable to single out evangelical Anabaptism as the truly significant stream and it is here that our interest is located.

At this point a modern analogy might come in handy. Evangelical Anabaptism may be compared to present-day restorationism, alias the house church movement (although this name is now distinctly out of date). Both are diverse phenomena. In this country there are at least eight networks of restoration churches and many other churches which have informal ties with them. Some of the latter are in established denominations. These networks have much in common, but are also distinct in theology, practice and ethos. Generalisations made from outside about the entire movement need to be treated with great care because of the internal differences, yet the tendency is for established denominations to treat a part as though it were the whole. Exactly the same happened to the Anabaptists, although perhaps with more excuse, in view of the lack of communication systems of the day.

Restorationism has similarities with Anabaptism that could be drawn out in detail to indicate that it is a movement in the Anabaptist tradition. It is operating with a free church understanding. A balanced treatment would also need to point out the differences. Many of the criticisms that were made of Anabaptism (sectarianism, perfectionism, intolerance, exclusiveness, literalism) are frequently made of restorationism, with varying degrees of undeniable accuracy in both cases. The development of this analogy must await another occasion and probably another writer. The point is that an examination of the present-day phenomenon may at least give the flavour of the Anabaptist revolution, although to be realistic, the imagination must go on to supply the society in ferment in which the Anabaptists were living and the vicious persecution which they endured.

With this impression in mind, a brief glance at the Anabaptists themselves may be helpful and we shall follow the suggestion of G.H.Williams by sketching briefly the evangelical

Anabaptist movements associated with Grebel, Simons, Hutter and Marpeck, inserting in their midst two further names, those of Balthasar Hubmaier and Michael Sattler.

Conrad Grebel (c 1498—1526)

Grebel is known as the chief founder of Swiss Anabaptism in Zürich and as the first man in the modern age to carry through the baptism of believers. He came from a wealthy Zürich family and had the advantage of a university education under humanist influence in Basel, Vienna and finally Paris, where he went off the rails morally and failed to complete his education. His conversion probably took place in 1522 and he became closely associated with the famous Zürich reformer Zwingli. He became concerned to study the word of God and apply it to the reform of the church as a friend and supporter of Zwingli.

This friendship came into great tension in October 1523 when it became clear in public dispute that Zwingli was not prepared to press ahead with thorough reform of the Catholic mass in accordance with his own teaching. Grebel and a group of about fifteen like-minded friends feared that for political reasons Zwingli would fall short of obedience to Scripture. They met together frequently for study and fellowship and sought to put forward compromise plans for the reform process, none of which were accepted. During this period, families in the outlying villages were beginning to refuse to have their children baptised, and interest in the subject of baptism increased until it became the cause of the final break with Zwingli.

Zwingli himself had previously preached against infant baptism, but on January 18th and 21st, 1525 the town council, under his influence, issued orders that Grebel and his associates must stop their activities and that all unbaptised infants be baptised immediately on pain of exile. Grebel himself had a two-week-old daughter. On January 21st at an illegal meeting of the group, Georg Blaurock felt impelled by the Spirit to ask Grebel to baptise him, and once this was done, himself baptised the rest of the company on confession of faith. Anabaptism was born and began to spread rapidly. By Easter, Grebel himself had baptised over 500 people and spent the next months alternately on the run, preaching and in prison, until he died of the plague in August 1526.

Grebel's closest supporters in these years were Felix Manz (1498—1527) and Georg Blaurock (c1492—1529). Manz, the illegitimate son of a priest, possessed a thorough knowledge of Latin, Greek and Hebrew and, like Grebel, emerged from the close circle around Zwingli. He was an eager preacher who, after his own baptism, was continually being arrested for baptising. He was sentenced to death on January 5th, 1527 and executed by drowning in the fast waters of the River Limmat, the first Anabaptist martyr to die at the hands of Protestants. Blaurock was a fiery character and a forceful evangelist who was formerly a priest and possibly a monk, although evidence confirming this is lacking. He arrived in Zürich at the time when events were coming to a head and was the first person to receive believers' baptism. His career is one of aggressive evangelism and harassment from the authorities culminating in his execution by burning on September 6th, 1529.

Balthasar Hubmaier (c1480—1528)

Hubmaier was the reforming priest of the church at Waldshut, some twenty miles from Zürich, and he too was a friend of Zwingli. He held a doctorate in theology and was known as a fine orator. At Easter 1525, he and his entire congregation were baptised and became Anabaptist. Hubmaier became the foremost apologist for believers' baptism in his written works. Against the majority Anabaptist opinion, he held a more positive view of the state and of the magistracy, believing that they could serve the gospel. This distanced him from other groups, but has meant that Baptists, who reflect this position, have regarded him highly and even considered him the hero of

Anabaptism. He moved to Moravia in search of liberty and attracted many others because of his teaching ability. Eventually, he was tried on the rack for heresy in Vienna and, without recanting, was burned at the stake on March 10th, 1528. A few days later his wife joined him in martyrdom when she was thrown into the Danube with a stone tied around her neck.

Michael Sattler (c1490—1527)

Sattler was a learned man, acquainted with Scripture in its original languages, and was a Benedictine monk in a monastery near Freiburg in south Germany. Through studying the Scriptures he rejected the monastic life, left it, married and took up employment as a labourer, but persecution drove him to Zürich in 1525, where he joined the Anabaptists and preached in their cause. Forced to leave, he moved to Strasbourg and debated with Martin Bucer, the Reformer of that city, on the nature of the church and its discipline, gaining his respect but not his agreement in this process.

Evangelistic work in the area of Rottenburg prepared the way for his involvement in the first major conference of Anabaptists at Schleitheim, over which he presided in 1527 and from which emerged a confession of faith which laid a foundation of agreement for the growing numbers of southern German and Swiss Anabaptists. Sattler's overriding concern was for the establishing of a holy church. Eventually, he was arrested and tried along with his wife in Rottenburg. After being horribly tortured he was burned at the stake on May 20th, 1527. Eight days later his wife was drowned in the River Neckar. The public reaction against his death was considerable, not least from Martin Bucer, who described him after his death as 'a dear friend of God'.

Pilgram Marpeck (d 1556)

Marpeck emerged as the leader of Anabaptism in south Germany and was a native of the Tirol, Austria. He came from a prominent family and was a mining engineer, holding a responsible position which he was to lose in 1528 for refusing to co-operate in catching fellow Anabaptists. He moved to Strasbourg where he became leader of the Anabaptists. He worked in the city forests and later as a brilliant town engineer, through whose ingenuity the whole town was to prosper. He had an excellent intellect and initially was highly regarded by the town Reformers, until he publicly disagreed with them. His engineering ability at first gave him protection from imprisonment but eventually he was forced to leave and to exist for some years as an itinerant teacher. From 1544 to his death in 1556 he worked as the city engineer in Augsburg. Marpeck was one of the finest minds produced by Anabaptism and the most able exponent of its emerging free church theology.

Jacob Hutter (d 1536)

Hutter originated as a hat maker in the Austrian Tirol. He was probably baptised in 1529 and was set aside for the service of the gospel. Because of severe persecution, he organised the staged migration of his congregation to Moravia in search of freedom, and eventually moved there himself, becoming the leader of a community seeking for a permanent home. He possessed exceptional organisational skill and used it to found a distinct movement. This group was to become that branch of Anabaptists who have practised community living and even today are called Hutterites. They are found now largely in North America as a consequence of migration. Hutter himself returned to the Tirol after 1535, was captured, tortured and burned to death on February 25th, 1536. His wife was executed two years later.

Menno Simons (c 1496—1561)

Menno is the Anabaptist leader who laboured to reorganise the Anabaptists of the Low Countries in the wake of the disastrous rebellion at Munster and consequently lent his name to their descendants, the Mennonites. In 1524 he was ordained priest at the age of twenty-eight in Utrecht, and came only reluctantly to Anabaptist convictions. Through Luther's writings he slowly became convinced about the priority of Scripture. After hearing about the martyrdom of an Anabaptist, he searched the Bible and became convinced that believers' baptism was scriptural. Yet it took the disaster at Münster to move Menno's heart to such a degree that he felt impelled to become the shepherd of the leaderless flock. He left the Roman Catholic Church and took to an underground existence as a voluntary evangelist that was to last for the rest of his life. By seeking out the believers, he became known as a capable and devoted leader and was received as an elder. The task Menno performed was an apostolic one of gathering, tending and teaching the church and it is largely down to him that the northern wing of the Anabaptist movement was saved from collapse and rebuilt on biblical foundations. Unusually for one who had been pursued for years, Menno died of natural causes in 1561.

The object of these short sketches is not to give an exhaustive account, but to paint pictures of the kind of people who were involved in the emergence of Anabaptism. Many other portraits could be given of leading figures and thousands of others who shared their faith and their courage. Further investigation would reveal that there were differences of thought and theology between those we have already encountered and that not everything about them might appeal.

Grebel, for instance, exhibits in the little that we have of his writings a literalist and wooden approach to Scripture. Sattler seemed to have an unrealistic notion of the perfection that was achieved in the believer through the new birth. Menno was definitely off-beam in some of his teaching on the Incarnation. These elements were often corrected by later generations of their followers. Other features that may act as a warning to us will be indicated in due course.

We need, however, to remember that most of these leaders only lived for a short time after their baptisms, that much of that time was spent on the run or in prison and that they were continually living in fear of harassment or exposure. These are hardly circumstances which make balanced theological reflection possible, although they may be conducive to grasping certain insights with remarkable and unshakeable clarity. It is to these insights that we must give particular attention, because in it their contribution is to be found. In the rest of this chapter we are concerned to reflect upon some interpretations of the Anabaptist movement, to investigate its connections with the English Baptists and then to draw together some of the ways in which it might serve us today by way of inspiration and of warning.

Interpreting the rise of Anabaptism involves asking two questions: where did it come from, and what is its essence? We shall notice that there are three basic answers. The first is the view, common among Mennonite historians and theologians of this century, that Anabaptism is a completing of the Reformation. From this perspective we are to look for the beginnings of Anabaptism in the Reformation itself, which took the lid off certain issues and restored the Bible to its position of central authority in the life of the church in the localities where it held sway.

The early Reformers, such as Luther and Zwingli, sought to work out their theology consistently from the Bible and succeeded in emphasising the primary doctrines of Scripture alone, faith alone and grace alone. In their early insights, both spoke language that the Anabaptists would whole-heartedly have endorsed.

Luther outlined a picture of a church composed of believers, meeting together for mutual upbuilding, and worshipping simply, practising the priesthood of all believers. Zwingli had severe words to say against infant baptism. But both of them drew back from their earlier radicalism. They realised as they went on that society as they knew it would be deeply threatened if they continued on this course and that the signs of anarchy were already present. Each of them, and they were followed in this by Calvin and the English Reformers, continued to endorse some form of sacral state.

The genius of the Anabaptists therefore was that they took the Reformation to its logical conclusion. They brought church, state and baptismal practice under the critical judgement of the Bible and found each of them lacking. Unlike the Reformers, they did not hold back but were prepared to challenge and reject the sacral state, whatever the cost to themselves of obedience to their convictions. This interpretation of Anabaptism as the logical extending of the Reformation principle has a great deal to commend it.

It is certainly the case that in Zürich, or in the experience of Menno Simons, as examples, the teachings of Luther and Zwingli were stepping-stones into Anabaptism for those previously involved in the Roman Catholic Church. It must be remembered that the Zürich circle emerged from the Bible study groups that came into being under Zwingli's influence and encouragement. It is also significant that some leading theologians of the Reformed tradition have more recently been following the principles of the Reformation to their conclusion and saying quite plainly that the Reformers' arguments against the Anabaptists were unconvincing.

Karl Barth, for example, adopted a congregational understanding of the church and argued for the practice of 'responsible', that is believers', baptism. Emil Brunner spoke up for the concept of the gathered church, or *ekklesia*, against an insitutional view. Both of these thinkers developed their opinions from a consistently Reformed basis rather than in dialogue with Baptists. More recently, Jurgen Moltmann has re-affirmed broadly similar conclusions. The progression of such as these adds weight to the view that the Anabaptists were simply being more consistent than the mainstream Reformers and that they are well understood as the left-wing of the Reformation.

A second interpretation looks elsewhere for an explanation. This is the view that Anabaptism represents a bubbling to the surface of subterranean forces which have been present in the church since the fourth century. Once legalised, the institutional church began to accommodate to worldly power, and corruption set in. The other side of this was that an alternative church began to develop which was closer to the evangelical simplicity of Christ and the apostles and which existed as a protest against the establishment. Monasticism belonged to this protesting tendency, with its attempts to build within the institutional church a voluntary community of the truly committed. Medieval renewal movements and the various anticipations of the Reformation, in people like Hus and Wycliffe, also belong to it.

This alternative stream of devotion, which had been driven underground by persecution, erupted to the surface once the changes of the Reformation period made it possible. Some writers have thought to find in this alternative church a line of continuity back to the apostles. This seems contrived and unnecessary, but the existence of an unformed, and perhaps at times chaotic, alternative church history is not to be denied. The linking factor between these movements, rather than an alternative apostolic succession, is more likely to be an instinct which leads believers back to the fountain-head of their faith in Christ and constantly insists on obedience to him against the corruptions of the established church. As long as a corrupt church endures there will be those who, under the influence of the Spirit and the word of God, rise to protest against it.

According to this second line of interpretation, the Anabaptists are not the children of the Reformers but their step-children. Their true parentage is to be found further back in the church's story. This too is a plausible interpretation of the emergence of the movement.

A third possibility awaits us, namely the view that Anabaptism has its roots in the monastic experience and is a form of laicised monasticism whereby monastic values are made accessible to the ordinary person. The most striking example of this possibility is Michael Sattler, the former Benedictine monk who was burned in 1527 and was largely responsible for the Schleitheim Confession. Comparison of Sattler's writings with the Benedictine rule reveals many similarities. The Benedictines were concerned to construct a biblical lifestyle, placed great emphasis on following Christ and stressed the obedience of faith. Understood in this light, baptism which is freely entered into corresponds with the monastic vow which binds the monk to the life of obedience in community.

In Anabaptism, baptism was voluntary submission to the discipline of the church 'in the perfection of Christ', that is, in maintaining the purification wrought in the believer through the new birth. This helps us to understand why church discipline and the brotherly union of the church were such important issues for the Anabaptists. Sattler was not the only monk to become an Anabaptist. We have already seen that the early leaders included not a few priests and it should not surprise us that elements of Catholic devotion that were deemed consistent with the Bible entered into the Anabaptist movements to a greater or lesser degree.

As we previously noted that Anabaptism was a diverse phenomenon, so we may now note that the forces that brought it into being were also diverse. The three strands of interpretation we have outlined each indicates part of a total picture which is more complex than any one of them on its own. They indicate tributaries of the broad river which was to become Anabaptism. No doubt there were others. We may think of medieval mysticism or of the social and economic forces which were leading to protest, sometimes in violent fashion, against the oppression of the peasantry.

It is the variety of factors involved that may account for the interest which is currently being displayed in the Anabaptist movements by many who are able to identify with aspects of its ethos. But notwithstanding its Protestant and Catholic inheritances, we should recognise that here is a movement which decisively broke with both and went beyond them in its

willingness to pursue its objectives by the power of martyrdom and sacrificial love, rather than by force and the sword.
There is one incident, the Münster rebellion, that may seem
to contradict this, and yet it can be shown to be not truly of a
piece with the evangelical Anabaptism that we have been
investigating.

Because of its diverse origins there is much that evangelical
Anabaptism may have to say to contemporary religious and
social interests. For those who are interested in the renewal of
the church, the convergence of various streams of renewal in
Anabaptism is striking and strengthens the conviction that it
may function today as an inspiration to renewal. Our attention turns at this point to a further question that has been
hotly debated, as to the nature of the links between continental Anabaptists and English Baptists.

First of all it is worth asking why we need examine this
subject. The answer is that our origins help to define our
identity. Opinions among scholarly Baptists have diverged
strongly over the part Anabaptism has played in their own
story. In the seventeenth century, Baptists were keen to
defend themselves against the charge of being Anabaptists for
two reasons. They regarded the word, which literally means
rebaptiser, as a false description since they believed in one
baptism, but the baptism of those who believe and not of
infants. Also, after the Münster rebellion, the charge of Anabaptism was tantamount to a charge of sedition and they were
keen to show that, although demanding religious toleration,
they were in every respect good citizens.

Popular attitudes to Anabaptism since that time have
tended to be determined by how Baptists wished to view
themselves in the present. In times when their self-estimate
has been more conservative, they have played down or even
denied the connection. At other times, they have felt themselves to be more radical and have wanted to retrieve their
Anabaptist and separatist roots. In general, the current view
seems to be that, basically, the rise of the English Baptists can
be satisfactorily understood as a development of separatist,

Puritan religion in the England of the sixteenth century, without reference to the continent.

But Anabaptist influence upon this movement is likely to form part of the broader picture for the following reasons. Although the origins of early English separatism are obscure, the first gathered churches appeared in the middle of the sixteenth century in Kent and East Anglia, where there were colonies of Dutch refugees, some of whom were known to have been Anabaptists. It is possible therefore that separatism itself developed as a result of Anabaptist influence, since as the historian E. A. Payne put it, 'Ideas had legs in the sixteenth and seventeenth centuries, as they have today.'

It is beyond doubt that the first Baptist church founded in 1609 in Amsterdam and led by John Smyth was influenced in this way. The church met for worship, and many of them lodged as well, in the large bakehouse of a leading Amsterdam Mennonite, Jan Munter. In 1609, Smyth baptised himself, in the absence of a person accepted as qualified to do so, in this same bakehouse and then proceeded to baptise his flock. It would seem likely on the face of it that he did not come totally independently to this conviction but may have been helped in his movement towards it by contact with the Mennonites. This possibility becomes a probability when we consider that he baptised himself by affusion, or pouring, which was the Mennonite method of baptism.

Further, as the months passed, he began to show himself in agreement with distinctive Mennonite teachings, such as the christological views of Menno Simons. Indeed, the General Baptists, who have their origin with this group and who were the first to advocate the gathered church, believers' baptism and freedom of conscience in this country, commonly manifested in later years some of the distinctive doctrinal positions of Dutch Anabaptism.

Furthermore, Smyth became convinced that he had been wrong to baptise himself and submitted himself for baptism in the local Mennonite church. This action caused a division in his own church and a part of it, under Thomas Helwys, returned to London to start there the first Baptist church on English soil, in Spitalfields. Those who remained with Smyth were eventually received into membership of the Mennonite church and after his death in 1612 became absorbed into it. His name and those of others of the group are today honourably recorded on the wall of the Mennonite church on the Singel in Amsterdam.

This evidence would appear to be sufficient to prove the positive assertion that Anabaptism played its part in influencing the rise of the English Baptists (as illustrated by Smyth) and the negative assertion that the Baptists do not owe their origin completely to them and are distinct (as illustrated by Helwys). The judgement of E. A. Payne would appear to be sound:

> The religious life of the seventeenth century was like a tumultuous sea, blown upon by winds from several directions. That one strong current of air came from the Anabaptist movement of the previous century I am convinced. Nor need Baptists be ashamed to admit it... To speak of 'harm' and 'unhappy consequences' if there is any recognition of a connection between Anabaptists and Baptists seems to me to be historically unsound. It also implies an unjust reflection on a very notable movement to which all the churches of the modern world owe a debt. [13]

Despite this historical discussion and whether or not a substantial linkage can be proved, the basic similarities of Anabaptists and Baptists may be determined in theological terms. Both movements stood for the believers' church, believers' baptism and freedom of conscience. At the very least, then, we are faced with two movements reading their Bibles under roughly similar circumstances and coming to parallel conclusions. Both movements exhibited in their early years a breadth and flux of opinion (compare the early Anabaptists with the Baptists of the Civil War period) which was only to settle down in the course of time. Apart from considerations of historical causation, there is here a theological similarity which enables Baptists to see that they belong together with

the Anabaptists in the same family of spiritual life and aspiration. Their witness and heritage is something that we need to
reclaim for our own benefit.

So we come finally to seeing Anabaptism as a source for
renewal in our own day and to the question of what we may
learn from it and how it may inspire us. My suggestions are as
follows:

Anabaptism has something to teach us about discipleship

It must be understood as a movement of radical discipleship
which took seriously the theme of following after Jesus. This
must be seen against the background of Reformation teaching, which centred upon a rediscovery of justification by faith,
that is, the doctrine that sinful men and women are made right
with God by trust in the work of Christ apart from any effort
of their own. Without denying this truth the Anabaptists
believed that the Reformers, Luther specifically, stressed it to
the point of neglecting the need to follow after Christ in life.
Characteristically, they would stress regeneration, the new
birth wrought in the heart by the Spirit and leading to a new
life. From this they went on to argue for Christian obedience
expressed in baptism and disciplined living within the
believers' church. These distinctive doctrines need to be seen
as following on from the life of discipleship.

In this sense, the Anabaptists stand today as a witness
against those forms of evangelical religion which see 'getting
saved' and 'going to heaven' as the core of Christianity and
which reduce discipleship issues, how we should live once we
are saved or as we are being saved, to matters of secondary
interest. The danger of this is that Christian experience risks
being manipulated in the service of ideologies which are in
direct conflict with the spirit of Jesus. That this happens where
discipleship is made secondary rather than primary is evident
from the ways in which evangelical religion has been captured, in part and at various times by British imperialism,

American nationalism and other forces which seek to co-opt it into the service of the status quo.

The Anabaptists remind us that faith has to do with the *obedience* of faith (Rom 1:5) and that life in the midst of the community of disciples is an integral part of this.

Anabaptism has something to teach us about evangelism

It has been tempting to include something in this book about evangelism and to speak of it as a prime value and commitment among Baptists. After all, the Declaration of Principle of the Baptist Union states in its third article that 'it is the duty of every disciple to bear personal witness to the Gospel of Jesus Christ and to take part in the evangelisation of the world'. It is certainly the case that in other parts of the world Baptists are keenly evangelistic and that in Britain we number the pioneering missionary William Carey among our forebears.

This said, I am not convinced that Baptists have been as intrinsically and keenly evangelistic as they like to think. Sometimes, the demands of evangelism and discipleship can seem to be in conflict; concern for a community of true disciples, that is, for quality, can appear more important than concern for evangelism and growth, that is, for quantity. The Anabaptists appear to have held together great zeal for both.

This was illustrated by the first baptisms of January 21st, 1525, when the participants on that occasion immediately went out to preach and convert and were to be found in the fields, villages and homes, preaching and baptising, until imprisonment or martyrdom caught up with them. The evangelistic zeal of the Anabaptists is particularly evident in what came to be known as the Martyrs' Synod, which took place in Augsburg on August 27th, 1527. Sixty leading figures in the movement came together to establish a definite programme which they proceeded to carry through by sending out missioners. They expressed a firm determination to proclaim the doctrines and ethical principles they regarded as right and not to be deterred from it by persecution or death. One article records:

> The conference appointed missionaries, who went out in all directions in twos and threes to all the countries where their fellow disciples lived, to teach, comfort and strengthen them, or to build new brotherhoods. Their speech was so impressive that frequently a few hours sufficed to establish a new congregation. Of their converts they demanded an upright life; when a brother sinned he was to be admonished, and if he was in need he should be aided by the brethren; anyone who was unwilling to do this should not request baptism. Their opponents were surprised by the rapid spread of the movement. Unable to understand it, they asserted of some of the preachers that they carried little flasks of a magic potion, which they passed around through the audience to put a spell upon them.[14]

It is plain from this that the Anabaptists were intensely evangelistic and that something akin to revival conditions was being experienced, both in the emergence of the congregation in Zürich and its vicinities and in the subsequent growth of the movement. Since they controlled no political units, their only way to growth was through evangelism and it was the Great Commission which was the spur. It has been pointed out that the Anabaptists were the only group in the Reformation to do this. The Reformers themselves were not evangelistic, since they followed the principle that the ruler determines the religion of his people. For the sake of evangelism, Anabaptist missioners were prepared to forsake home and family, lead a nomadic existence and, in thousands of cases, to give themselves in a martyr's death which itself might serve to spread the evangelistic fire. In the longer term, the toll of martyrdoms succeeded in extinguishing the fires. As an example of their phenomenal success we may cite the Dutch evangelist Leenaert Bouwens (d 1582) who baptised, according to his own diary, 10,378 people across northern Europe.

Anabaptism can teach us something about zeal

This is a quality not always welcome in Baptist circles—indeed, it is sometimes looked on with suspicion and cynically when found. The zealous are automatically regarded as being either naive or obsessional. Yet the Anabaptists were consumed by zeal for the house of the Lord and it is this which made them capable of immense and awe-inspiring acts of heroism. In some areas, special Anabaptist-hunters were recruited to track down and execute them without even a trial. The *Martyr's Mirror* lists 800 Anabaptist martyrs by name and it is conservatively estimated that over 4,000 met a martyr's death at the hands of Protestant and Catholic governments alike. They were strengthened by their conviction of being on the right road as revealed by God in Scripture and by their acceptance that following Christ attracted the hatred of the world.

Yet it is unjust to describe them as fanatics. The attitudes revealed in their letters written from prison demonstrate that they were tenderly concerned for their families and deeply aware of the price they were being called upon to pay for Christ's sake. Such martyrdoms lasted into the seventeenth century and imprisonments for longer still. The courageous example of these people is hardly surpassed anywhere in the history of the modern church and has only a few parallels in English Baptist history. Its enduring value is as an example of profound conviction set on fire by the Spirit and demonstrating a sustaining power greater than that of which human beings are ordinarily capable.

Anabaptists can teach us something about the way of peace

Their understanding of following after Christ meant that they were prepared to adhere to his teaching even if they did not always understand the reason for their action. This is noticeable in their refusal to swear oaths. The reason they gave was that Jesus forbade it and they do not seem to have penetrated into a deeper rationale.

Following Jesus also meant the rejection of violence, since he was the Prince of Peace and had given specific commands in this regard to his disciples. Their stance was all the more surprising in an age which relied upon violence to compel conformity more routinely than is the case today. In spite of the huge amount of cruelty shown to them and their loved ones, they consistently responded by loving their oppressors and forgiving them. Here we see the emergence of the first so-called 'peace church', which was followed in the next century by the Quakers. This witness was a sign that they were prepared to follow Christ even to the point of what would be seen as a dangerous nonconformity. It took place at a time when any able-bodied man might be called upon to defend the borders of his province or city and signals a civil disobedience for the sake of Christ.

The meaning of this witness for the ethical stance of those who live in a nuclear age, and whose governments still have power to unleash immense destructive potential on others, needs to be pondered long and hard. In principle, it shows that the Anabaptists clearly understood how obedience to Christ has social and political, as well as personal, implications. And they were not afraid to follow Christ to the extreme limit against the requirements of Caesar. The experience of salvation which they had known embraced the forgiveness of their sins, the transformation of their lives, membership in a new community and an ethical position that set them apart in the world, and probably required more courage than participation in many wars.

Negative lessons from the Anabaptists

The positive Anabaptist qualities we have outlined may well serve the renewal of the church in our own day and are worth pondering and emulating. Other, negative qualities may serve as a warning to us lest we repeat them. It must be said that these are not all uniquely Anabaptist but are also reflected in the mainstream Reformers, that many Anabaptists were scarcely given opportunity to rise above them and that some of these negative elements were called forth by the extreme measures that were employed against them. They do tend, however, to be the shadowy side of the kind of religious life for which Anabaptists stand.

At times they exhibited a biblical literalism which failed to see the Bible in the more nuanced terms it requires. They were capable of being very severe in their judgements upon others and of exhibiting an inner violence, despite their rejection of actual violence. This in turn suggests that their idea of sanctification was sometimes narrowly conceived. Their ideas of the church lent themselves to becoming sectarian, legalistic or perfectionist. Their practice of church discipline, especially that of the ban, by which the unruly were shunned by the church, has overtones of psychological violence.

The most important criticism of all is that they were apt to miss the element of 'friendship with sinners' in their search for the true and faithful church. This is a trenchant criticism because this element is one of the most evident and startling aspects of the way of Jesus Christ, which the Anabaptists were seeking to follow in life and death. Incidentally, it shows that in Jesus a reality was present that far exceeds the normal behaviour, even religious behaviour, of human beings. The insight that the church is open to sinners is a crucial corrective to much that they might have been inclined to do and teach, and is of course to be applied to many other ways of being the church that differ considerably from that advocated by Anabaptism.

A significant feature of the modern scene is the renewed attention and new respect being given to Anabaptists in a number of quarters. This chapter has attempted to indicate how the movement might serve us all in the present, not just those who stand in the tradition of the believers' church. The modern world has anticipated the demise of the sacral state by slowly killing it off. It is a pity that this was not done by the church as a voluntary act many years ago, but then power once held is difficult to relinquish. In this post-Christian, pluralist age it may very well be that renewed attention should be paid to the Anabaptist movement, both by Baptists and other free church folk and also by Anglicans and others who are seeking to come to terms with a new situation.

Anabaptism provides models for church life in an age when nominal Christianity is bound to decrease and true faith must come into its own. As once it was like a 'strong wind' blowing upon the 'tumultuous sea' of the seventeenth century, so may it be again. Although the Anabaptist movement belongs to history, the Anabaptist vision belongs to the present and to the future, and is able to inspire us and help towards the renewal of all the church in the service of Christ.

IO

Towards Transformation

The final decade of the twentieth century looks set fair to be a more than interesting time. The arrangements of the human calendar are, of course, largely a matter of convenience and there is no intrinsic difference between this time and any other. Time will continue to be the unrenewable resource it has always been in the fallen condition of humanity. Yet the thought of being in the last decade of the twentieth century is dramatic. No doubt we shall be treated by the media to lengthy reviews of what has happened in the last thousand years and informed of where we have come from. We shall be reminded that what we are now is the sum total of all our previous experiences.

More awe-inspiring than dramatic is the recollection that at the end of the decade we shall be turning a corner that leads not only into the next year, decade or century but into the next millennium. We shall be the first people in a thousand years to have had this experience. The thought of it produces a feeling of insecurity, because while we are able to look back upon the past and recognise it as familiar, even with its blemishes, the future has not yet been lived and is uncharted. It brings with it no feeling of familiarity or security; we are reminded of the immense potential of the human race for good or evil, to help create or destroy, and any thoughtful person will be certain to ask 'If this is what we have done with the past, what are we capable of doing in the future?'

On a universal scale, the next ten years are likely to contain sustained reflection on the meaning of life, its direction and the values by which we must live. The explosion of new age mentalities and the search for contemporary spiritualities give testimony to this. In Christian terms, this presents us with the opportunity to move with the apparent turning of the spiritual tide in the 1980s and to work for the reclamation of men and women for God. The use of the decade as a time of sustained evangelism is to be welcomed because it is thoroughly appropriate.

Another factor comes into this which has yet to be widely commented on. The next decade will see the two thousandth anniversary of the birth of the Man from Nazareth, in whom Christians believe God was uniquely and savingly present. Because Jesus was actually born during the reign of Herod the Great according to the Gospel record, and Herod is known to have died in 4 BC, we must date the birth of Jesus at around 6 BC. In a very few years therefore we shall be celebrating the two thousandth anniversary of his coming and drawing the attention of people back to him. In the coming years, there are marvellous opportunities awaiting us, both for evangelism and for us to return to Jesus as the author and finisher of our own faith.

The threat of an insecure future will very possibly rekindle in many Christians the sense of the nearness of the end. The apocalyptic parts of the Bible may well be reconsidered as giving us clues to the meaning of world events and the shortness of the time that remains. The perennial inclination of those who take the Bible seriously to express the sense of spiritual urgency in terms of shortness of time is well represented in history and in the Bible itself. When the awareness of ultimate and critical realities pressing down upon this present world is sharp, it is not surprising for it to be expressed in terms of the Day of the Lord coming as a thief in the night.

Every Christian must live in a state of readiness, conscious that this could be the day or the hour of God's coming to us again in Christ. This is how the first believers lived and it is apparently how Jesus taught them. One imagines they would never have dreamed that history might last for another 2,000 years.

While it is entirely right for us to live conscious of the imminence of Christ's coming and to cultivate a spirit of readiness to meet him, we must join this with a further attitude. Because we do not know the day or the hour, we must also be prudent. Jesus tells the parable in Matthew 25:1–13 of the ten virgins who went out to meet the bridegroom at the wedding feast. Because 'the bridegroom was a long time in coming' (v5) they fell asleep, and when they woke to trim their lamps for the bridegroom's arrival, five of them (described as 'foolish') found they had not brought enough oil, having expected only a short wait. The point is that although we may expect the coming of the Lord to be soon, we must also take the long-term view and be prudent. Our destiny may involve a marathon rather than a short sprint.

These two attitudes, continual readiness and a wisdom which looks to the long term, are paradoxically joined in the wise Christian. If history teaches us anything, it is that it is full of unexpected surprises. While hoping for the fulfilment of history in the coming of the Lord, we must also reckon with the possibility, startling though it might be to some, that we may yet be only at the beginning of the history of the church.

This is unaccustomed thinking for evangelical Christians, who are always apt to think that the present generation is the last. Yet it is a train of thought worth following. When we imagine that we are approaching the end of time, we look back upon the church's history and see in it a catalogue of successes and failures. We are hard put to explain the failures in a people who boast of redemption. But if we think of the past as that which has been lived through and recorded for our instruction, we may gain a different perspective. The failures of the past are there to instruct us in the present. They are part of the growth in understanding and wisdom which can come when we learn from our mistakes. The past may help us then to *learn how to be the church* both in the present and in the future in which the fullness of our story and mission is yet to come.

The argument of this book has been that the Anabaptists and Baptists laid hold of certain basic insights about being the church. From them the whole church may learn, but, in order to be a prophetic witness, those who see themselves as heirs of this legacy must consciously re-appropriate it and live it out. It is not enough to imagine that because the time is short all we must do is save souls. Because the coming of the Lord may be delayed, we must also be busy about building the kinds of colonies of heaven on earth that are best able to represent him here and now and do his work.

History teaches us that the work of evangelism, of people being won to faith in Christ, and the wider mission of which evangelism is a part, are effectively forwarded by those who are committed to the free church principle. When those in established churches catch the evangelistic vision, it is not least because they have begun to think as free church folk and have given up the notion, embraced even by the Reformers, that the state determines the shape of religious commitment. The growth of the church, understood in free church terms, is entirely dependent upon the evangelistic activity of its members. There is a direct line of continuity between the emergence of the free church principle and the development in subsequent centuries of the missionary movement which led to the geographical spread of the faith. The re-appropriation of these principles today will produce an impetus in evangelism for the good of the human race.

If we are indeed at the beginning rather than the end of the church's history, renewing the Baptist way of being the church is essential for the future work of evangelism. It is the burden of this book that Baptist identity is of more than secondary importance, more than a mere composition of non-essential optionals. Rather there is something of the gospel in it which, once neglected, adversely hinders the mission on which we are sent.

In the Preface, I made reference to three current factors which will help shape, however modestly in some cases, the next decade of life in the West. These were the reconstruction of Europe in the wake of the collapse of Marxist-Leninism; the appointment of a new Archbishop of Canterbury to lead the Church of England (and other branches of the church as well) through the decade of evangelism into the next millennium; and the shifts and changes in style, resources and leadership with which the Baptist Union enters that same period of history. I wish to indicate how these realities could be connected.

By chance, I recently came into possession of a journal published in 1977 which contained what it called 'an alarming graph', charting the decline of the Baptist Union since its high point at the start of the century. The last sentence of the supporting comment was: 'At the present rate of decline, extinction will take place in 1989.' It was the kind of critical publication which seemed to take a perverse delight in its prediction. Perhaps therefore I might be forgiven for taking an equally perverse delight in the fact that it was wrong.

Actually, observation of the Baptist scene indicates that, while there are still black spots, there is also much life being expressed—in thriving churches, innovative projects, church-planting, new buildings and widespread local community involvement. Nearly all the Union's associated Theological Colleges are reporting increased numbers of applications from people who may be judged to be better educated and more experienced than at any previous point. The new leadership of the Union enters into its task at a time when the tide has visibly turned in the 1980s, as some predicted it would do, and when the common and institutional life of the Union is beginning to show the marked effect of the change in mood. Predecessors in the leadership role have brought the Union through some climactic changes, symbolised in the move to new premises which set the scene for marked and immediate changes.

The prospect which is before us is that of denominational renewal and renaissance. The opportunities are great. They need to be grasped.

It is essential that at a time such as this there should also be a theological renewal to accompany and guide the process of change. By this is meant not only a new consciousness in the churches and colleges of the importance of theology in general in interpreting and shaping our experience, but also a new awareness of the value of our heritage and its direct relevance for the sake of mission to our present situation. Theological education is not only for aspiring pastoral leaders but for all God's people. The Theological Colleges have an important task to fulfil in making theological enquiry both accessible to a wide number and passionate and committed in its expression. We have received from our past a depth of theological awareness which is an enviable resource and which should be built upon to produce a denomination in which theology is on fire and spiritual enthusiasm is theologically astute.

Yet the prospect of denominational renewal needs to be hedged around with reservations. Lesslie Newbigin has questioned the place of denominations in the mission of the church because he sees them as being themselves the product of the Enlightenment culture that we are seeking to make Christian. One might question whether Newbigin's negative analysis of the Enlightenment is the best interpretation of it and whether the privatisation of religious faith which he sees as its consequence is not rather the result of the Constantinian shift of the fourth century, of which he is far less critical than he ought to be. This said, his point stands. Denominations need to be relativised. Whereas churches must of necessity exist in supportive and missionary groupings if the notion of the Church Catholic is to have any cash value (this is what the notion of association signifies—we cannot, after all, relate equally to all other congregations), it is tragic when this becomes denominationalism, the fragmentation into groups which close themselves off from each other.

For this very reason, denominational renewal must take

place within the context of ecumenical commitment, by which I mean, not the exalting of particular and limited institutional forms as all-important, but the overarching commitment to the growth in unity of all who name Christ as Lord. The New Testament is clear about the potential of Christian unity in forwarding Christ's mission. This too will be a feature of the coming years and will grow in significance for Baptists, not least because the new Archbishop is one with whom they can the more readily identify.

Ecumenical process is about giving and receiving. If Baptists have a distinctive witness, it is not for themselves alone but for all the church. The principles of which we have spoken at some length are capable of wide adaptation and the prospect begins to open up of Anglicans, Catholics and others moving towards an expression of these principles in ways which differ in externals from those which we know, but are recognisable as being of a piece with them. Already this may be seen taking place in, for instance, the base communities of South America or the grass-roots renewal of the Catholic Church in North America, to say nothing of what is now visible in a myriad parish churches in our own country. The reverse side of this is that there is much whereby we ourselves might be enriched, as we in our turn receive the distinctive witness of other parts of the body of Christ. Some of our own lacks in spirituality, prayerfulness and fullness of congregational life will be made up as we receive gratefully what is offered.

The need to make known our own witness and discern that of others once more highlights the need for theological awareness in our ranks. Clearly, many theological questions in the ecumenical process remain unresolved and should not be avoided, but it is no longer these which are the chief obstacle to growing together. By its very nature, the sense of an interchurch process moves away from the idea of one monolithic church towards that of a forward-moving diversity of traditions which are nevertheless recognising in one another

the presence of the Christ. The church from its very beginnings in the New Testament has been diverse and yet with a
unity, because of its central focus in Jesus Christ. The chief
obstacle now is the distinction between those who believe the
faith and those who have retreated into a doubting nomi-
nality. The difficulty for Baptists will come, not when they
encounter others who are different but who clearly and sincerely believe, but when they encounter others who, though
Christians in name, appear not to believe in what they pro-
fess.

The renewal of Baptists is thus to be placed within the
wider context of the whole church, in which the renewal of
faith in Jesus Christ as the Son and Word of God must
increase. We have a crucial part to play, and in giving will
receive back more than we give.

Yet all of this is still preliminary. The church of Jesus Christ
must be seen in its central role as the bearer of the kingdom of
God. We are not to look to the political process for the
coming of a kingdom which engulfs but transcends this present order. Its consummation lies beyond history. But we look
for signs of that future in the political transformations which
are possible in the present. We have already indicated how
the political health of our society owes much to the emergence
of the free churches. The liberties we enjoy today are at least
indirectly the result of their action. We are not saying in this
that the early free churches necessarily had a political programme or intention. Their intention was to live according to
Christ. The fruit of their obedience in political terms was far
greater than they might have imagined or guessed.

There is a principle involved here. Where people make it
their intention to live as disciples of Christ, the creative
impact of this action in social and political terms exceeds even
that of which they are aware. John Howard Yoder expresses it
like this:

The political novelty which God brings into the world is a community of those who serve instead of ruling, who suffer instead of

inflicting suffering, whose fellowship crosses social lines instead of reinforcing them. This new Christian community in which the walls are broken down not by human idealism but by the work of Christ, is not only a vehicle of the gospel or fruit of the gospel; it is the good news. It is not merely the agent of mission or the constituency of a mission agency. This is the mission.[15]

Not just for the sake of evangelism but for the sake of the well-being of society, it is vital that the church learn how to be the church in the way which accords most fully with Jesus Christ. It is this task which awaits the whole church, and the part which Baptist believers have to play in it is the reason for the challenge which this book poses. It is not a hole-and-corner concern which only affects the domestic policy of a medium-sized Christian denomination in Great Britain. It has to do with life for the world.

The cataclysmic changes in Eastern Europe which took us all by surprise are instructive for us. Liberation from oppression and totalitarianism is always possible. In particular, the part played by the church in its various guises should not go unnoticed. For years the church has been a vehicle of conscientious resistance to an alien and dehumanising philosophy. In Jesus Christ, men and women have found a resource and a ground for resistance which has meant that even while being captive they were inwardly free. That organised existence which we call the church allowed people to be shaped and changed by a radically different vision of reality and then, when the time was right, became the vehicle of a new order coming to be. There is a picture here of the way in which the church as the new community becomes an agent of social change.

Of course, in democratic societies the same process is at work, with the major difference that it is by no means as obvious what the church is called to resist, when it is greeted more with apathy than hostility. The need for theological and spiritual discernment is all the greater when the opponents of the gospel do not announce themselves as such. Yet God's way remains constant. His way is not, as is assumed by more conservative Christians, that of changing individuals to the point where they are able to change society. This is only part of the truth. Certainly they do need to be changed and personal conversion is a crucial element in the church's mission. Yet such an approach can still leave many assumptions, prejudices and injustices unchanged for the reason that they belong to the fallenness of the group rather than the individual. God's way of social transformation is to use a social structure to change other social structures. That social structure is the church, the community of men and women who are learning Christ together and introducing into society a new power which liberates and humanises.

Granted that the church itself is sometimes captive, it nevertheless, in so far as it focuses upon Jesus Christ, has a self-asserting resource which enables it to be self-critical and to advance beyond its present failures. Where Christ is at work, the possibilities of rethinking are always present. There is a continual task of prophetic, theological and spiritual enquiry which must take place within the church to enable it to be true to its calling to be free for Christ.

One example of how all of this may work is drawn from recent Eastern German Baptist experience. In Buchow near Berlin, the East German Baptist Seminary may be found. In that town, in the process of rediscovering democracy, the president of the seminary, another staff-member and the pastor of the small Baptist church became respectively the president of the city parliament, the mayor and the assistant mayor, directly involved in the shift to a new way of political existence. The reasons for their elevation to such prominence were twofold. First of all, they were recognised as folk who had kept their integrity through the years of totalitarian domination. Having been part of a community shaped by following Christ, they were able to resist the pressure to conform. But secondly, membership of the local Baptist church had enabled them to develop vital skills in decision-making and relating which the bulk of the population, by virtue of its bondage to political passivity, had either lost or never acquired. These proactive skills made the Baptist church a natural resource for the rest of the community when the time of liberation came. Baptist leaders are now serving others by enabling them to find and express the skills which they themselves gained as a result of their social existence in the fellowship of Christ.

In similar ways, not just Baptists, but all God's people, not just in Eastern Europe, but in all places, may serve the transformation of their societies in anticipation of the final day of freedom. It is to that end that the transforming of the church of which we have here spoken is directed.

Our final task is to relate a modern-day piece of prophetic symbolism as witnessed and perceived, not by myself, but by another. In recent years, the Baptist Union of Great Britain held its annual Assembly in Leicester, in the centre of England. One evening was given over to a multi-media presentation of the work of home mission, the ministry of evangelism and church-planting to which the Union gives invaluable support. By all accounts, the evening was excellently conceived and executed and folk were held in rapt attention, as the initiatives being taken and supported were described and news of progress and encouragement shared.

As the presentation drew to a close, a marvellous thing happened. In the lights of the large hall where the meeting was taking place, a beautiful wood-pigeon began to fly above the heads of the audience. It seemed at first as if it could be part of the presentation and folk might have thought of the dove of the Holy Spirit, who alone can inspire and enable the effective mission of the church. In fact, it was a spontaneous and unplanned occurrence, but of the most appropriate kind, symbolic of God's desire to use and equip Baptist believers, churches and structures by the Spirit for his work. People left the meeting in enthusiastic mood.

But on returning the following day, they found that the wood-pigeon was still in the hall and that through the night it had been seeking in some distress a place where it might come to rest and find a home. It was now clear that it was trapped, imprisoned by the building. With difficulty, it managed in time to find a place to rest and, out of sheer exhaustion, went to sleep. What had begun as a spontaneous piece of symbolism ended with an air of tragic sadness.

Perhaps we are entitled to see in this something deeper. The Holy Spirit is brooding over Baptist churches and their denomination, seeking somewhere to rest and fulfil his mission. Yet we imprison him within our attitudes, traditions and structures and fail to allow him to express through us the life and power which reaches out. We grieve him by our unwillingness to change and be changed, and the consequence is not that the Spirit falls asleep, but that his work among us is quenched. We must see that it could all be so different and that by taking up the challenge to change, Baptist churches and associations of churches could become a major means of the Spirit's transforming activity. As we take up for ourselves the challenge to be transformed, we shall surely fulfil the transforming mission on which we are sent.

Notes

1. G. H. Williams and A. M. Mergal (Eds), *Spiritual and Anabaptist Writers* (Westminster Press: Philadelphia, 1957), p 74.
2. *Baptist Union Directory 1990–91* (Baptist Union: Didcot, 1990), p 9.
3. *ibid*
4. W. T. Whitley, *A History of British Baptists* (C. Griffin and Co: London, 1923), p 20.
5. Cited by R. G. Torbet, *A History of the Baptists* (Hudson Press: Philadelphia, 1950), p 25.
6. *Baptist Union Documents 148–1977* Ed. R. Hayden (Baptist Historical Society: London, 1980), p 7.
7. Karl Barth, *Church Dogmatics* Vol IV/2 (T and T Clark: Edinburgh, 1958), pp 680–681.
8. Cited in J. F. V. Nicholson 'The Office of Messenger Amongst British Baptists in the Seventeenth and Eighteenth Centuries' *Baptist Quarterly* Vol xvii (1957–58), p 206.
9. *ibid*, p 207.
10. Leonard Verduin, *The Anatomy of a Hybrid* (Eerdman: Grand Rapids, 1976), p 11.
11. G. H. Williams and A. M. Mergal, *op cit*, p 80.
12. D. W. Bebbington, *The Nonconformist Conscience: Chapel and Politics 1870–1914* (George Allen and Unwin: London, 1982), pp 11–12.
13. E. A. Payne 'Who Were the Baptists?', *Baptist Quarterly* Vol xvi (1955–56), p 342.
14. H. S. Bender, article 'Martyrs' Synod' in H. S. Bender et al (Eds) *The Mennonite Encyclopaedia* Vol iii (Mennonite Publishing House: Scottdale, 1957), p 529.

15. J. H. Yoder 'The Believers' Church in Mission' (unpublished paper delivered to the Conference on the Concept of the Believers' Church, 1967), pp 30–32.

Select Bibliography

Bebbington, D.   *The Nonconformist Conscience: Chapel and Politics 1870–1914.* George Allen and Unwin: London, 1982.

Dunn, J.D.G.   *Jesus and the Spirit: A Study of the Religious and Charismatic Experience of Jesus and the First Christians as Reflected in the New Testament.* SCM: London, 1975.

Dunn, J.D.G.   *The Living Word.* SCM: London, 1987.

Dunn, J.D.G.   *Unity and Diversity in the New Testament: An Enquiry into the Character of Earliest Christianity.* SCM: London, 1977 and 1990.

Durnbaugh, D.F.   *The Believers' Church.* Macmillan: London, 1968.

Estep, W.R.   *The Anabaptist Story.* Eerdman: Grand Rapids, 1975.

249

Fiddes, P.S.   *Charismatic Renewal: A Baptist View*. Baptist Union: London, 1980.

Fiddes, P.S.   *A Leading Question: The Structure and Authority of Leadership in the Local Church*. Baptist Union: London, no date.

Gish, A.   *Living in Christian Community*. Herald Press: Scottdale, 1979.

Hudson, W.S.   'Who were the Baptists?' *Baptist Quarterly*. Vol XVI (1955/56) pp 303–312.

Kreider, A.   *Journey Towards Holiness*. Marshall Pickering: Basingstoke, 1986.

Moltmann, J.   *The Open Church*. SCM: London, 1978.

Moltmann, J.   *The Church in the Power of the Spirit*. SCM: London, 1977.

Newbigin, L.   *The Gospel in a Pluralist Society*. SPCK: London, 1989.

Newbigin, L.   *Foolishness to the Greeks*. WCC: Geneva, 1986.

Newbigin, L.   *The Other Side of 1984*. WCC: Geneva, 1984.

Payne, E.A.   *The Baptist Union: A Short History*. Baptist Union: London, 1959.

Payne, E.A.   'Contacts between Mennonites and Baptists.' *Foundations*. Vol IV (January 1961).

Payne, E.A.   'Who were the Baptists?' *Baptist Quarterly*. Vol XVI (1955/56), pp 339–342.

Richards, L.O.   *A New Face for the Church*. Zondervan: Grand Rapids, 1970.

Sellers, I.   'Edwardians, Anabaptists and the Problem of Baptist Origins.' *Baptist Quarterly*. Vol XXIX (1981/82), pp 97–112.

Snyder, H.   *New Wineskins: Changing the man-made structures of the church*. Marshall, Morgan and Scott: London, 1977.

Snyder, H.   *The Community of the King*. IVP: Downers Grove, 1977.

Snyder, H.   *Liberating the Church: The Ecology of Church and Kingdom*. Marshalls: London, 1982.

Torbet, R.G.   *A History of the Baptists*. Judson Press: Philadelphia, 1950.

Underwood, A.C.   *A History of the English Baptists*. Baptist Union: London, 1947.

Verduin, L.   *The Reformers and Their Stepchildren*. Paternoster: Exeter, 1964.

Verduin, L.   *Anatomy of a Hybrid*. Eerdman: Grand Rapids, 1976.

White, B.R.   *The English Separatist Tradition*. OUP: Oxford, 1971.

Williams, G.H.   *The Radical Reformation*. Westminster Press: Philadelphia, 1962.

Williams, G.H. and Mergal, A.M.   *Spiritual and Anabaptist Writers*. Westminster Press: Philadelphia, 1957.

Wright, N.G.   *The Radical Kingdom*. Kingsway: Eastbourne, 1986.

Wright, N.G.   *The Church*. Scripture Union: London, 1984.

Yoder, J.H.   *The Priestly Kingdom*. Notre Dame University Press: Indiana, 1984.

Kingsway Publications

Kingsway Publications publishes books to encourage spiritual values in the home, church and society. The list includes Bibles, popular paperbacks, more specialist volumes, booklets, and a range of children's fiction.

Kingsway Publications is owned by The Servant Trust, a Christian charity run by representatives of the evangelical church in Britain, committed to serving God in publishing and music.

For further information on the Trust, including details of how you may be able to support its work, please write to:

> The Secretary
> The Servant Trust
> 1 St Anne's Road
> Eastbourne
> East Sussex BN21 3UN
> England